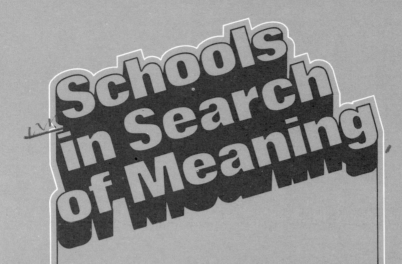

Schools in Search of Meaning

**Prepared by
the ASCD
1975 Yearbook Committee**

James B. Macdonald and Esther Zaret
Co-Chairpersons and Co-Editors

Association for Supervision
and Curriculum Development
Suite 1100, 1701 K Street, N.W.
Washington, D. C. 20006

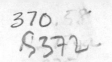
Contents

iii

Acknowledgments

Final editing of the manuscript and publication of this booklet were the responsibility of Robert R. Leeper, Associate Secretary and Editor, ASCD publications. The technical production was handled by Elsa Angell, with the assistance of Nancy Olson, Teola T. Jones, and Maureen Montgomery, with Caroline Grills as production manager.

The photographs on pages 6 and 24 are by Michael D. Sullivan. The photograph on page 150 is courtesy of the Smithsonian Institution.

Foreword

READING THIS BOOK is an unsettling experience, much like having to look at one's self in a mirror while under the glare of a spotlight. It is a probing analysis of the particular interests of people involved in the schools. The essays here are the product of an ASCD "think tank" in which six persons searched for meaning not only for schools but for themselves and ourselves in relation to schools. Each person wrote and rewrote in the area that seemed most important to him or her. The working papers created along the way, but absent here, could also have provided a volume of interest and significance to us.

Here we see ourselves—educational writers and practitioners— as good-intentioned people but working in conflict with one another on many issues and at odds with and critical of the shortcomings of our public. Consciously or unconsciously we seem bent on preserving the present class structure of society. The section which establishes context recaps the long history of criticism of the American schools that has tended to swing between two poles, focusing either on something wrong with the schools and the individuals in them or something wrong with society. Questions of the human relationships of schooling, the major and unique functions of education and society, the interests of specific groups, mechanisms of domination, present contradictions, and potential partnerships and alliances in the common tasks of restructuring society and schooling are among the fundamental issues raised by these authors. The book is a call to its readers to join in a cooperative search for new forms and new meanings for schooling.

Dwayne Huebner confronts us with everyday manifestations of hidden means through which schools provide a setting for individuals to control other individuals. He cites examples of deliberate limitations placed on possibilities for children within the school.

A thorough, searching analysis of the four-faceted problem of women and schooling is sharply brought into focus by Esther Zaret. We are charged with pondering the concept that power elites among women may dominate, manipulate, and oppress members of their own dependent group for selfish personal interests.

From this, we move directly to William Burton's unforgettable piece. His provocative satirical commentary exposes the raw stuff that goes into the everyday life of the school. Another discomforting jolt to our self-assurance is the contradiction between the professed ideals of the schools and the quality of life in everyday practice as revealed to us by James Macdonald. Probing still deeper is Steve Mann's examination of the contradictions in society that are reflected in the schools. He provides us with a look at the societal reality of a ruling class dominating the oppressed classes of America, at how we got that way, and at how the schools maintain this situation through control of ideology, control of knowledge, and control of training for the work force.

Ethical dimensions of our accepted ways of viewing students are analyzed by Michael Apple. Labeling of students with such terms as "poorly motivated," "slow learner," "underachiever"—terms tinged with value judgments—is practiced by individuals in the school toward those who are different. Labeling, accompanied by nonacceptance of modes of inquiry, reflects the schools' adherence to past perspectives and concern for efficiency above the importance of the personal lives of students. He challenges school people to take up the torch of advocacy of students' rights.

The concluding section of the book outlines specific actions to be taken. The professional work of educators can enter new realms of meaning aimed at ending the oppression of youth if we can understand and develop true democracy for teachers and students in the schools, if we can develop a curriculum that reveals to students the nature of dominant socioeconomic structures rather than one that indoctrinates for passivity, and if we can form linkages between education and the political struggle of all dominated persons.

I recommend this book to you for serious study and consideration followed by curriculum action toward new meaning for schools.

University City, Missouri   GLENYS G. UNRUH, *President 1974-75*
November 1974   Association for Supervision and
    Curriculum Development

Introduction*

"SCHOOLS IN SEARCH OF MEANING" was the general topic assigned for the Yearbook of 1975. To fulfill this charge, the appointed editors selected an initial Committee of people who enjoyed a long history of personal and collegial friendships, shared a core of common professional interests and commitments, and freely acknowledged their areas of ideational disagreement. It soon became apparent in our deliberations that we ourselves were educators "in search of meaning" and that the meaning of schooling in American society is the other side of the coin. Some very critical decisions were made in the early meetings of this group.[1]

We recognized that implicit in our charge were three fundamental problems:

1. That schools no longer appear to mean what most of us hoped they would mean in American society;

2. That the development of relevant personal meanings in schools is a precarious and doubtful endeavor; and

* The introduction was drawn from the face to face dialog and copious written exchanges among the Committee members over a three year period. Regretfully, we can include here only a minimum of the ideas and opinions explored.

[1] For example, the Committee assumed that the readers of this Yearbook would be familiar with the basic empirical school-related data that have been accumulated over the past several years. We refer, for example, to the "Coleman Report," the Mosteller and Moynihan reanalysis of these data, Jencks's *Inequality*, Boocock's *An Introduction to the Sociology of Learning*, Goodlad's *Behind the Classroom Door*, and the ASCD-sponsored study on "Oppressive Practices in Schooling." Our collective awareness has included and builds on these kinds of data.

1

3. That the search for meaning in our professional lives and activity should be a function of all educators.

It became apparent in the Committee's deliberations that all three of these problems were intricately related to one another. It was clear that writing a yearbook with this theme would be an extremely difficult and soul searching experience. The Committee was faced with two basic approaches to the task. The first and most typical response would have been to develop some outline of topics to be covered and then locate appropriate persons to contribute to the volume. Then, a collected set of papers reflecting different aspects of individual interpretations could be compiled and presented to the Association. The first year began with this format in mind.

It soon became apparent, however, that the complexity of the three problems did not allow for any reasonable breakdown of topics that would provide meaning for the professional activity of the Committee, or that seemed to shed new light on the social and personal meanings of and in the schools.

The meaning of schools clearly appeared to arise from the dialectic of the meaning of schools in society and the facilitation of the quest for personal meaning in schools by students and professionals. There was no bridge that we could see between personal and collective meanings in the existing traditional conceptions and analysis that we were engaging in and becoming more acutely aware of. Our problem as we saw it was to attempt to define or create a social opening into which novelty might erupt.

In this sense the Yearbook became a consciousness raiser for the six Committee members. As we met and engaged in a common effort to probe, reflect, criticize, and analyze our personal meanings, a common consciousness began to emerge which became the device needed to create a conceptual bridge between individuals, between personal and institutional discourse, between social and organizational forces, and between technical and political action. We began to feel that for better or for worse we were committed to a collective search for meaning which necessitated the collaboration of our initial Committee as the exploratory writing team in search of meaning.

It was decided by us at that time that the usual pattern of selecting authors, the idea of "balance" between public school and university, minority and majority groups, was simply not feasible if we were to accomplish our task. We recognized our decision as a potential limitation, but a necessary one if we were to create enough unity to develop a collective position.

The various efforts of curriculum writers of the past few years (including our own) were attempts, we felt, to create or develop more powerful ways to think about schools. As curriculum people we seemed no longer to have a common base of thought, hence the proliferation of individual schemes. Though obviously a necessary step, individual efforts, we felt, became self-defeating after a time. We needed, we believed, to attempt a collective effort that had some grounding in history and a common set of analytical tools. We did not take for granted that we had the historical skills necessary for the task, nor for that matter did many (if any) curriculum people. Yet we could not turn this job over to the "historian" without, again, losing our collective thrust.

Further, to ask educational historians to do this task for us would be to sanction the work of the curriculum person who only thinks of the present, and hence is encouraged to think techno-logically. Thus we did the best we could to become at least sensitive to the historical context from which we spoke.

Our first efforts were directed at clarifying our individual and collective positions by addressing ourselves to the topics listed below. The Committee responded to this common charge in highly diverse ways.

1. *Standing out*—that is, our individual views of (a) man; (b) society; (c) tradition, culture, knowledge; and (d) nature of values (value theory), or grounding our argument, if you wish, in proposing our own value position. We asked that *everyone* write a short state-ment of his or her stance on these matters. We probably would not use the term but this would be our "Poetics" section.

2. *Standing under* (or understanding—this section would be our hermeneutic (won't use the word again) attempt to do two things: analyze the present state of schools and criticize this state from our value positions. Each of us must do this job alone since each of us has a frame of reference that is personal and different. The big job would be to put this section together.

3. *Standing in* (or with)—this would be our section on politics (should we use the term?). Not that "politics" can be left out of all of it, but that in a restricted sense, this section would be prescriptive of direction, formats, practices, program, change approaches, etc., that would follow from our analysis and critique in light of our values.

In our early position "papers," it became clear that we were collectively concerned about power and justice and that we shared a practical concern for education, in the sense that politics and ethics, the "shoulds" of human prescriptions, are central to the meaning of schools and persons. We agreed that most curriculum talk is confused about modes of valuing and motives for talking, that the moral and political modes must be emphasized, and that we should be conscious of the need for groups, perhaps yet unformed, to affiliate for the sake of holding power and providing the conditions for justice.

While we were committed to the paramount importance of a political focus in our discourse we were also aware that the foundation of this discourse was grounded in the spiritual underpinnings of the Judeo-Christian (and other) religious traditions. On the whole then our political discourse is spiritually bracketed (at least implicitly) in the desire to strive, through the political integration of action and reflection, for the primacy of the person as person and not as thing.

The Activity of Liberation

It seemed to us that the "real" meaning of schools (as they presently stand) is their depoliticization as an institution. We felt that we must help expose the fact that some people use schools, books, and ideas to control others; and that life is being aware of controlling and being controlled, of the oppressed and the oppressors. Thus we felt we must call attention to political freedom, not simply existential freedom. Schools, we felt, are not in search of meaning, only people are. Meaning is always the meaning of particular people with particular interests and with particular histories. We avowed to try not to do anything which legitimates attempts to hide behind rhetoric that masks individual self interest or the interests of others. Thus political analysis is our attempt to break out of the control of a status quo which permits superficial changes in order to prevent any basic change in perception and control.

Education is the activity of liberation (à la Nietzsche): liberation from ignorance, fear, want, disease, and alienation from oppression, and liberation from the role of unwitting oppressor. Anything short of this overreaching goal is an act of training, and an act of present depoliticized training in the interests of others.

The present training endeavors that pass for education are not neutral. The schools have mistakenly thought that their practices, activities, and aims were value free (or they were free from having to commit themselves to values). These misguided "centrist" tendencies have actually resulted in the acceptance of broader moral values that destroy the development of personal meaning and are representative of a form of oppressive social meaning.

Much more dialog took place and it would be remiss not to suggest that certain areas of disagreement were not resolved. It was never clearly agreed upon whether the concept of "class" should be construed in strict economic-social terms or broadened to "class interests" in terms of a power elite. In either case, "In whose interests?" was a commonly heard question. Meaning also cannot be totally reduced to political terms. The spiritual dimensions, or if one wishes, the metaphysics of politics, are morally complex and varied. Whatever accord the individuals held was based upon the sense of justice, personal integrity, self-determination, and freedom that are a common historical background for us all.

In the end we spoke as many voices, reaching out for the areas that seemed most important to each of us, but grounded in a consensus, analytical framework, and a sense of urgency that we hope will come through to the readers. We were six friends with much in common who explored what was important to us and tried to resolve our new found divergencies. We did not totally achieve one voice to express our collective consciousness but we did experience excitement and growth in the search.

In this introduction the editors have paraphrased and quoted liberally from selected portions of the written and spoken dialog of the six members of the Committee over a three year period. In some ways this book might better have been an unedited collection of the dialog and letters. The responsibility for the total impact of this introductory section is, finally, the work of the editors.

Section I
CONTEXT

Our Perspective

IT HAS BEEN OUR EXPERIENCE with colleagues in the education profession that persons in professional education—whether teacher, supervisor, administrator, or professor—are filled with good intentions. As a general rule, we have been impressed by the concern for young people, the devotion to task, and the expressed commitment to humane values. There is no doubt in our minds that the vast majority of educators possess a strong desire and intent to serve their fellow people. We share these positive intentions.

Yet there is, we believe, something awry in schooling processes, wherever they take place. Our practices do not fulfill our desires, our good intentions, our humane ideals. There would appear to be an area, a sort of "no-man's-land," that we are unable to cross in order that our ideals may be realized in practice.

A frequently expressed reason for the gap between good intentions and unacceptable results is "they won't let me." Teachers say administrators or supervisors won't let them do what is best. Administrators often blame the board of education. Sometimes the identification of "they" extends downward including, at times, the young people we presume to educate. All too often, the "they" is an almost completely unidentified group. When we search for the precise "theys" who do not allow us to work in the manner we desire, it becomes extremely difficult to determine exactly who "they" are or how the blocking process takes place.

Yet, identifying and attacking the "they" is a popular activity among educational writers as well as among educational practitioners. Unfortunately, the writers are no more precise in identifying the "they" who impede the translation from ideal to practice than are the practitioners. In general, however, both writers and practitioners seek to explain the impediment of ideal into practice by identifying either groups of individuals or political forces which find embodiment in groups of individuals. These individuals, groups, and/or forces seem at odds with each other.

The criticism which identifies the "they" as individuals or groups of individuals is often couched in psychological language and identifies a very immediate or personal "they." For instance, some critics find the "they" who prevents "us" from acting out our good intentions to be "unprepared" or "disadvantaged" students. Other critics lay the blame on the doorstep of "mindless" or "ill-prepared" teachers and administrators. Some critics even find fault with "unconcerned" or "reactionary" publics, or "uncaring parents." These criticisms are frequently of a personal nature, growing from the personal experience of the critics. The implicit assumption is that the solution to the problem is for a particular group to become more aware of its actions, recognize the problems caused by such actions, then modify their actions to bring about what ought to be.

The criticism which explains impediments to the realization of ideals by political forces also speaks of groups, but in more impersonal and global terms. Groups such as the conservatives, liberals, establishment, church, or business community are sometimes accused. In these criticisms, however, the language used is the language of power—a sort of naive political language. The assumption of these critics is that "they" know what they are doing, that "they" are doing wrong or acting from narrow interests and must be prevented from doing so. Often these critics have an "us" which should replace the "they" as the group in power. Sometimes these critics are merely suggesting a realignment of power balance.

These critics frequently see the political as overlapping the personal. They recognize that persons embody and create political forces. They offer a more richly detailed description of the "they" than the purely personal critics. Nevertheless, even political critics offer seemingly rational proposals which assume that understanding and awareness lead to removal of impediments. If a group or an individual understands that which intrudes between ideal and practice, then the two can be made to coincide.

Critics infrequently point to yet another dimension of the groups and circumstances which define schooling activity. This dimension is the economic. Critics who deal with the economic issues usually do so to provide motives for political behavior or to shift the identity of "they" to the taxpayers or government. Seldom do critics attempt a thorough economic analysis of why schooling practice seems to deviate so consistently from the professed intentions of school people.

Looking at the many faces of "they," we must conclude that, in a very real sense, Pogo is right in claiming "We have met the enemy, and they is us." At some point someone is looking at us (you and me) as the "they" who won't let them; whether we be teachers, parents, administrators, teacher educators, or just taxpayers. We believe that "they won't let me" is a normal (though simplistic) human response to the wrong questions about schooling. Both the questions and the response reflect a limited perspective on education, one that ignores the dialectic nature of the social, political, and economic realities of our society. From this limited perspective "they" becomes an amorphous, shifting conglomeration of groups and circumstances that slip away just when we feel we have our fingers on the problem.

As we see it, the pressing need is for an alternative perspective, one that can generate effective educational criticism leading to constructive educational action. It is this task, the articulation of such a critical perspective, that we of the 1975 ASCD Yearbook Committee have set as our task. In our perspective the data of present educational practices are not problems that can be solved by naming "theys," changing school practices, or working with families and individual children. On the contrary, we believe that the data which reveal massive inequality in the educational process are proof that the system is working well.

Class Interests Influence Schooling

We believe that schools in our society constitute a given set of meanings; we are concerned with identifying how those meanings promote the interests of certain power groups and systematically keep other groups powerless. We believe that domination of the interests of one class over another constitutes oppression in schooling; we are concerned with illuminating the structures and mechanisms of that oppression. Because of our dissatisfaction with prevailing modes of criticism in dealing with these issues, our group, with varying degrees of commitment, has turned to an analysis of schooling based on class interest.

A major premise of this Yearbook is that the identification of class interests in schooling provides both a unifying analysis and a guide to action. For example, through the use of such analysis we can show that Silberman's "mindlessness" is a disguise for a very mindful set of class interests, and by so doing can show the relationships among the offensive school practices that to him are merely a list of various misfortunes. We can show that the chaos of the various school reform movements can be overcome by educators who accept class interest as a fundamental determining factor in our institutions and who can declare unequivocally which set of class interests is theirs. The Yearbook is an attempt to demonstrate these contentions.

We are aware that our attempt to utilize class interest in educational criticism is not the first such attempt. We acknowledge and respect the work of George Counts, John Childs, and their followers who made some attempts to apply class analysis during the 1930's. We believe, however, that these attempts, as useful as they have been, were doomed to failure from the beginning.

Cremin has suggested that the Social Reconstructionists failed in their task because they failed to link their work with the parallel work of other groups outside the school. No doubt this contention has some explanatory power. We suspect that the failure of the Social Reconstructionists, especially as they attempted to use class analysis to guide their action, was for a very different reason. This reason was the failure of commitment to follow the analysis wherever it led. In short, had the Reconstructionists rigorously applied a class analysis, and had they followed the path illuminated by this analysis, their actions would have been clearly outside those considered legitimate by the liberal educational establishment, and largely outside actions considered legitimate by political groups not in the schooling establishment.

As a result of this failure of commitment, the Reconstructionists prostituted the class analysis, or, in the words of one of John Childs' students, they used "the class category in a random and arbitrary manner rather than in the strictly socioeconomic sense as conceived by the Marxists. It appears that (the liberal educators) conceive the class more as a convenient logical category than as a dynamic sociological reality." (In: Zalmen Slesinger, *Education and the Class Struggle.*)

It would be less than accurate to suggest that the writers in this Yearbook are clearly unified in their definition of "class" and "class interest." It is certain, however, that we all conceive "class" to denote a sociological and political reality, and believe that an analysis along the lines of this reality, however defined, is the only way in which the activities and meanings of schooling can be made to make sense. The crucial questions which will run through the writing here are, "In whose interest is it?" and "Who decides?" The answers to these questions outline different, but largely overlapping, notions of what classes exist in our society and how the interests of those classes work themselves out in public schooling.

Schools Legitimize the Present Social Structure

We begin with the assertion that the schools serve to legitimize the present social structure. The present social structure, called advanced United States capitalism is characterized by: (a) bureaucratic organization, (b) hierarchical lines of authority, (c) job fragmentation, and (d) unequal rewards. Fundamental to this system is the way individuals are allocated to the roles they will play in the hierarchy, and the justification on "objective" bases of unequal rewards. The schools serve this allocation function to a considerable degree. Education legitimates the social order by presenting a stance of objectively rewarding youngsters on measured cognitive achievement in the context of accepting the fundamental and critical nature of cognitive skills for success in the system.

Higher levels of schooling are considered the strongest determinant of those worthy of upper echelon jobs and higher rewards. Furthermore, it is important to convince both the "winners" and the "losers" of the legitimate nature of the status they have achieved through schooling. Thus through competition, success, and failure in the classroom, individuals are reconciled to the social positions they achieve.

Our critique is aimed at the analysis of schooling in terms of the social justice of its outcomes, not the equality of access to the system. Justice in this critique is focused primarily upon whether the present outcomes of schooling are necessary or natural phenomena or merely an epiphenomenon of a larger system.

From this "new" perspective, then, we plan to probe the counter forces of unidentified "theys" and provide a sharper analysis of the meanings of schooling in our society; uncover the myths and realities of these forces as expressed in contradictions in theory and practice of schooling; and, finally, provide an outline of concrete action points for people who wish to move together in transforming those forces.

We present our critical perspective in the context of a historical overview of criticism which has been concerned with identifying the "theys" who obstruct the enactment of humane ideals in schooling.

In the second section we present a series of individual critiques of schooling from an essentially radical perspective. It will be a mistake, however, to assume that each writer speaks with the same voice. We speak from common commitment and perspective, but "in many tongues." It is our hope that all of the presentations will incite you to further thought; but if not, that some one or more will provide you with a comfortable but growing awareness of the general perspective of this Yearbook.

The final section is an outline of action points for those readers who wish to join in the cooperative search for new forms and new meanings for schooling.

Criticism of American Schools

The history of American schools has been replete with criticism. It is an undocumented but accepted premise that in no other previous or contemporary society has so much been hoped for, asked from, given to, or taken on by the schools. Under such an assumption it is not difficult to understand why schools in America have been a focal point for criticism.

The American faith in schooling grew out of the American experience of mass education. The necessity for the rapid socialization of large immigrant populations, for establishing some common cultural denominators and commitment to the ideals of American democracy were early forces, to be followed by the social needs for rapid industrialization and social justice. On a personal level, education came to be seen as the major avenue for individual advancement and access to social mobility.

No other institution in American society was so well suited for its perceived integrative role as the public school. In a society where families were culturally diverse, churches multisectarian, business and industry highly competitive and individualistic, the school seemed to have a potentially coherent and cohesive social and personal meaning. Given the perceived centrality of schooling in American life there is little wonder that criticism should be endemic to its history.

It is a mistake to think of criticism only in terms of "critics," although admittedly in recent years certain individuals stand out predominantly in that light. The act of criticism, however, is engaged in from time to time by almost all of our philosophers and educators, and is implicit (if not explicit) in any movement or educational reform proposal.

Criticism has tended to swing between two poles, focusing at one end on what is wrong with the schools and the individuals within them, or, on the other hand, with what is wrong with society. The bulk of criticism has focused upon what is wrong with the schools. The criticism has been of five kinds: (a) schools are inefficient; (b) schools are socially and technically inadequate; (c) schools are inhumane; (d) schools are culturally inauthentic, and (e) schools are culturally authentic in maintaining the social-political-economic status quo of powerless groups in our society. The criticism of the schools in terms of what is wrong with society has appeared variously as Social Reconstructionism, Romantic Radicalism, and Political-Cultural Radicalism.

The educational establishment lacks historical perspective on the cycles of criticism directed at its practices and theories over the years. However, in *The Transformation of the School*, Cremin documents and interprets the origins and manifestations of criticism as they relate to his thesis of the rise and fall of Progressivism. An over-easy characterization of this criticism since the last decade of the nineteenth century through the turmoils of the twentieth century would be that criticism external to the educational establishment of practice was soon taken over by the so-called educational theorists, philosophers, or educational academicians. Later cycles of external criticism were then directed at both educational practitioners and educational writers. For instance, in the 1890's, a young pediatrician, Joseph Mayer Rice, traveled throughout the East and Midwest, visiting schools and talking with teachers, and wrote his devastating criticisms of public education in *The Forum*. Perhaps the one best known to educators was "The Futility of the Spelling Grind" (*The Forum*, XXIII, 1897), which indicated no significant correlation between spelling homework and competency as a speller.

The so-called progressive educators of the early part of this century, Dewey, Parker, the McMurrays, can be seen as critics of the practical status quo in education who asked the schools to do more for children than they were doing. The rash of progressive educators in the 20's and 30's, associated with universities, men such as Kilpatrick, Rugg, Bode, not only criticized existing school programs but quickly took the leadership in offering other theories and proposals for restructuring the curriculum and the schools. Other progressives such as Caroline Pratt, Lucy Sprague Mitchell, Margaret

Naumberg moved to demonstrate alternative educational procedures and curricula by setting up private schools. In the 30's, the criticisms were directed at the school as a potential vehicle for reconstructing the broader society. Certainly, Counts' pamphlet *Dare the Schools Build a New Social Order?* is well known to educators. The debates about social reconstruction that occurred in *The Social Frontier* among Childs, Bode, Dewey, and others also are an illustration of criticism within the academic circles of education which brings into question older practices and points in new directions. The concern for social reconstructionism was soon taken over by curriculum people such as Smith, Stanley, and Shores, in *Fundamentals of Curriculum Development*, to some extent by the proponents of CORE, and in modified and somewhat ameliorative fashion by the proposals of Stratemeyer, *et al.*, in *Developing a Curriculum for Modern Living*.

The lull in criticism associated with World War II was brought to an end by a variety of attacks from outside the realm of professional educators, criticisms which have continued into the early 70's. Lawrence Cremin chronicles and documents the early criticisms (Chapter 9). Nineteen hundred and forty-nine saw the publication of Daniel Bell's *Crisis in Education* and Mortimer Smith's *And Madly Teach*. Their criticisms were directed at the presumed lack of intellectual vitality of the schools, and the mismanagement of the educational enterprise by the professional educator. The attack against content continued with Robert Lynd's *Quackery in the Public Schools*, Arthur Bestor's *Educational Wastelands*, Paul Woodring's *Let's Talk Sense About Our Schools,* and Mortimer Smith's *The Diminished Mind*.

Criticism against the social orientation of the schools was reflected in the downfall of Willard Goslin as Superintendent of Pasadena's schools, a story told in David Hulburd's *This Happened in Pasadena*. This softening up process by outside critics led to a variety of external-internal actions which saw the cooperation of professional educators and outside organizations. The move to break the rigidity of school organizations came with foundation and industrial support for such programs as the ungraded school, television instruction, and differentiated staffing. The criticisms of the intellectual content of the schools combined with the launching of Sputnik was partially responsible for the Woods Hole Conference and Jerome Bruner's *The Process of Education* which soon became a tract for curriculum people. The focus upon the intellectual component of the school, pro and con, as well as the rigidity of the school as an institution, has produced much of the critical literature of the 60's and early 70's, identified with the names of Jules Henry, Edgar Friedenberg, John Holt, Paul Goodman, Charles Silberman, and Jonathan Kozol. The educational activists of the 60's and 70's have tried to duplicate the efforts of the activities of the progressive era by the establishment of communal schools, alternative schools, followed by the establishment educators who have tried to establish schools within schools or schools without walls.

ASCD's Criticisms of Schooling

In contrast to these trends the liberal explication of criticism in education of the 60's was capped in the publication of the ASCD 1962 Yearbook, an expression of urgent concern for the psychological well-being of the individual. The 1962 Yearbook, *Perceiving, Behaving, Becoming* was the most successful publication in the history of the Association. This Yearbook was received with considerable acclaim in educational circles, both within and outside the Association and still outsells by far any other of ASCD's hardcover publications.

This Yearbook was a powerful psychological statement and as such represents, from the psychologists' point of view, a critique of schooling that was the culmination of libertarian values. It spoke directly to the traditionally perceived role of ASCD as a professional organization on the cutting edge of humanistically oriented school practice and theory.

In retrospect, however, and with its worth still undaunted, the 1962 Yearbook appears to have been, not the harbinger of a new era, but the capstone of a past one. The future into which this volume was to speak proved to hold dramatic differences from the past out of which it drew its insights. Since 1962, the United States has encountered the social and economic turmoil of the civil rights movement, the peace movement, the student movement, the women's movement, the gay movement, and intense reaction to these phenomena. In short, the basically unified social perspective, which allowed ASCD to focus on naive consensus-oriented liberal notions of individual psychological needs of students, has been polarized to right and left. The strength of the volume, as demonstrated by Earl Kelley's "The Fully Functioning Self," Carl Rogers' "Toward Becoming a Fully Functioning Person," Abraham Maslow's "Basic Propositions of a Growth and Self-Actualization Psychology," Arthur Combs' "Perceptual View of an Adequate Personality," and other chapters, grew directly from assuming (as was vogue in the post-ideological society) that the great social problems were solved and thus the school could and should focus on individual problems.

If we have learned anything since 1962, it is that the individual is far more affected by social class, race, and ethnic status than by schooling, and that despite the liberal psychological rhetoric of school people, schools continue overwhelmingly to reflect and perpetuate the general economic and social arrangements of our society. In point of fact, the libertarian psychology of the 1962 Yearbook is clearly identifiable with the liberal tradition of United States politics which has failed to address itself adequately to the social and economic forces underlying the current and accelerating polarization of this country. Despite these obvious shortcomings, the libertarian psychological view of schools can and has become for many a religion and is, in a sense, an opiate of the educators (to paraphrase K. Marx).

By 1971, ASCD had been forced by social conditions to abandon the apolitical analyses of the past and attempt to explain more effectively the forces at work on the schools. The analysis adopted was aptly expressed in the title of the Yearbook that year, *Freedom, Bureaucracy, and Schooling.* No longer was the desired end of schooling adequately phrased in terms of psychological health or increased efficiency of the existing programs. In order for the humanistic thrust traditional to ASCD philosophy to be worked into schooling, it now was seen as necessary to defeat the bureaucratic complexity which schools had become. This volume marked a definite move by the Association into a political analysis of schooling. But the political analysis was often couched in the strange apolitical political language of the technologist, systems person, or liberal philosopher. With two notable exceptions, the chapters fell altogether too comfortably in line with Thomas A. Billings' "Alternatives and Innovations." Dismissing the recent criticism of schooling, particularly Paul Goodman and Edgar Friedenberg, as "negative, irrational, and strident . . . readable, marketable, and irresponsible," and yearning for the "sense of reason and balance" which "characterized earlier criticisms," for example, Paul Woodring and James B. Conant, Billings goes on to suggest that what is needed is a systematic federal approach to the problems of schooling.

The two bright lights in the 1971 Yearbook are the chapters by Herbert Kliebard and Donald Arnstine. Kliebard helps us to understand the political implications of the behaviorist thrust in contemporary schooling by tracing its roots to the scientific management theories of Frederick Winslow Taylor and the resultant efficiency oriented curriculum movement started by Franklin Bobbitt and his associates. Arnstine projects a future for educationists by reminding us that we have "isolated the pedagogical from the political dimension of education, studied the former, and forgot about the latter." He concludes his analysis of how freedom might be created in and by schooling with a forceful and direct statement:

> The educational bureaucracy will never *give* freedom to teachers, parents, and pupils, for this would call for a voluntary release of power. Historically, no group in power has ever just given it away. When power was lost, it was actively taken by someone else. But if freedom is to appear in education, it cannot result from the efforts of any single group. Freedom is not a possession that can be given by one group to others; it is a condition that exists when all groups share in making decisions. This sharing of power will result in educational policies that are more tentative, and in practices that are more flexible and alterable. It will also result in the disappearance of the educational bureaucracy, and its replacement by more numerous, smaller, local centers of policy making.[1]

Arnstine's analysis, however, leaves crucial questions unresolved. He locates the responsibility for the rigidity of schools—the lack of freedom in schools—directly with the school bureaucracy. He even goes so far as to claim that the bureaucracy controls the school board by its control of the information concerning any given situation. While this claim may be demonstrably accurate, it may also be largely irrelevant. What probably happens in the overwhelming number of cases is that the bureaucracy reflects and resonates the values of the board and, when discord does erupt, that the values of the board are usually fragmented but finally resolve themselves by coming back to base values which are also the values of the bureaucracy.

Finally, the 1971 Yearbook, while introducing the notion of political analysis, restricts the analysis largely to a political analysis of the school and does not attend to political analysis of the society and the political place of the school within that society. The result is that the school can be talked of as a "guidable system" à la Etzioni, and the assumption that all systems are basically "go" given some technical improvements. Despite this limitation the 1971 Yearbook was a powerful statement touching on many of the elements of the emerging radical critique of the 70's.

[1] Donald Arnstine. "Freedom and Bureaucracy in the Schools." In: Vernon F. Haubrich, editor. *Freedom, Bureaucracy, & Schooling.* 1971 Yearbook. Washington, D.C.: Association for Supervision and Curriculum Development, 1971. p. 28.

The political stance introduced in the 1971 Yearbook becomes more sharply focused in the accelerating criticism of schools in the 70's. In contemporary criticism of schooling the lines of criticism become less distinguishable in terms of social vs. educational critique. The school becomes the focal point for the synthesis of social criticism.

A Synthesis of Contemporary Criticism

Schools have ever been a convenient starting point for social critics, and have been subjected to this type of criticism as well as the criticism of school people interested in the institution for and of itself. The late 60's and early 70's have, however, been a time of even more pointed and intense popular criticism of the schools. This criticism has, in large part, grown out of the more general upsurge of criticism of all our institutions which, in turn, has been supported by both the civil rights and antiwar protest movements.

In the mid-70's, the major focus of criticism is with the failure of the schools to correct the plight of the "disadvantaged." The criticisms dwell on, or are concerned with, so-called cognitive qualities, an outgrowth of the criticisms of the 50's and the input of the cognitive psychologists such as Piaget and Bruner. They can be traced in lineage from attacks against the "life adjustment" concept of schooling (Arthur Bestor, James Koerner, etc.); through the structure of the disciplines (Jerome Bruner, etc.); into the mastery syndrome (Benjamin Bloom, etc.); down to the behavioral objectives (Robert Mager and James Popham, etc.); and back again to proponents of intellectual growth (Jean Piaget, Lawrence Kohlberg, etc.).

What these statements share in common is a set of assumptions that include as major points: (a) schools are essentially justified in terms of the cognitive growth of individuals, and (b) cognitive outcomes of schooling are determined primarily by the existing curriculum and the teaching that takes place in schools. Given these assumptions critics have set about in their various ways to right the anti-intellectualism of the schools by proposing the upgrading of school practices through a return to basic disciplines (and removal of frills), authenticating and reforming the basic disciplines, increasing the efficiency and effectiveness in producing cognitive outcomes, and developing programs to stimulate intellectual growth.

Measures of cognitive development are limited primarily to IQ and achievement test data (whether criterion referenced or general). Thus, the critical case for the cognitive position rests upon whether or not school practice can be the major factor in increasing intelligence or achievement.

The criticisms of the cognitive critics have been challenged by the geneticists, particularly Arthur Jensen and Richard Hernstein who have attacked the cognitive critics indirectly. That is, the geneticists' assumptions that IQ (and thus achievement) are differentially spread among races and social classes, and that "meritocracy" of genetic superiority is the natural order of things raise grave doubts about the cognitive commitment to "equal" education through school practices. On the contrary, Jensen feels that what is wrong with schools is that we are not differentiating school practice in order to teach an individual (or group) what he or she is most capable (genetically) of learning. Thus Jensen, and Hernstein as well, see the "failure" of compensatory education to be self-evident evidence that the cognitivists' approach is not a viable or sensible one.

Another group of contemporary critics may be classified as environmentalists. The environmentalists are often cognitively oriented. However, there are a host of "romantic critics" who are essentially environmentalists. These environmentalists are the liberal reformers of the current educational scene. At the heart of the environmentalist position is the conviction that equal opportunity will provide a just and fair system which allows youngsters to fulfill their potential. It is essential to realize that the environmentalist position is not concerned with equal outcomes (as many cognitively oriented critics are, for example, with mastery or behavioral objectives). Thus liberals argue that if we meet survival needs (Maslow), or if we give some people a "head start," or if we provide mental health, that is, if we remove the environmental conditions that deprive persons of an equal opportunity, then each person will fulfill his or her own potential in the system.

The data that concern all these critics may be summarized as follows: white and minority children of lower socioeconomic classes do badly in all school subjects, including arithmetic and reading. In reading they average two years behind the national norms. The lag is cumulative in that by the end of the sixth grade they average approximately three years below norms. The literature shows that poor performance is most closely related to social and economic class; however, segregated ethnic groups—in particular American Indian, Spanish speaking, and Black children—appear to do least well.

The cognitive critics would argue that we are not teaching well, that we are inefficient and ineffective in our practices, and/or that the content is trivial and anti-intellectual and thus not potentially stimulating of intellectual growth. Geneticists, on the other hand, would argue that this is the nature of reality. Upper classes have higher IQ's and higher IQ's lead to higher achievement. Consequently, the data above reflect a true picture of the genetic potential of the populations involved. Environmentalists would argue from a deprivation position. Lower socioeconomic class and minority children have been deprived of cultural and particularly critical language experience early in life and thus do not have equal opportunity to learn in school.

Cognitive, genetic, and environmental critics all begin with the tacit (or explicit) assumption that the present nature of the basic social structures is desirable. The data of present school practices are then explained and proposals for reforms made within the context of this overall acceptance. The call for greater authenticity of content, more efficient and effective procedures, differentiated programs, and programs to reserve equal access by doing away with "cultural deprivation," are seen as reasonable by these critics.

However, from the emerging radical social perspective, in its critique of schooling, these explanations and reform proposals appear to be missing the basic point, that is, that the explanations and proposals are all predicated upon an acceptance of the status quo in social stratification and serve to validate and legitimize, through schooling practices, the general social structures that now exist.

A More Radical Critique of Schooling

In 1974, a group of people using political language produced a Yearbook for ASCD that represents a move toward a more radical critique of schooling. This time a concern for freedom was expressed in the desire to create *Education for an Open Society.*[2] Again, however, the analysis did not seem to be powerful enough to probe to the root of the matter. The focus of the Yearbook, and the implicit definition of an open society, was the elimination of racism. Some of the contributions, notably that of Bruce Irons, went to the heart of the institutional racism of the school. But much of the

[2] Delmo Della-Dora and James E. House, editors. *Education for an Open Society.* 1974 Yearbook. Washington, D.C.: Association for Supervision and Curriculum Development, 1974. 224 pp.

writing again avoided the broader social, political, and economic foundations for racism.

Dan Dodson, in "Authority, Power, and Education," goes further with the analytical attempt. His suggestion that the social conditions which supported the "consensus model" of schooling no longer hold, and his proposal of a new "conflict model," are largely a logical extension of the earlier work of Arnstine. The new design which he proposed for schooling is roughly a design for political coalition in school decision making.

The power of Dodson's analysis is largely lost, however, when it comes time for the editorial committee to sum up in "Where Do We Go From Here?" The responses to the question are once again almost completely couched in action within the schools. The Countsian quality of Chapter 13's title, "Can Educators Help Create an Open Society?" is answered by the same type of political naiveté which marked the responses (usually curricular, in the narrow sense of the term) as good—if they could be expected to come about—but naive in the assumption that all that is necessary to bring them about is the determination and good intent of educationists.

A radical critique recognizes that each of the positions discussed issues from differing yet limited perspectives, none of which is satisfactory. In the view of the radical critic the fundamental reasons for the shocking educational data do not lie *in the children or in school practices* per se—but *in the society*.

While this approach to a synthesized radical criticism has often illuminated offensive phenomena with great clarity, it has not provided a unifying analysis that would both explain the problems and show us how to act upon them from a unified school-society perspective. While radical criticism of the 60's and 70's has identified a new "they" in answer to who is messing up the schools, it has backed out of the political implications of the radical perspective by failing to expose the special interests being served by the schooling practices they criticize. The criticisms have generally been individualistic and romantic, rather than systematic.

Social criticism, however, has more deeply rooted foundations and greater analytic power. Richard Bernstein, in *Praxis and Action*,[3] states that criticism "has the power not of delineating some utopian ideal which is to be striven for, but of revealing to men a critical understanding of what they are suffering." Unless criticism

[3] Richard Bernstein. *Praxis and Action: Contemporary Philosophies of Human Activity.* Philadelphia: University of Pennsylvania Press, 1971.

does this it becomes idle speculation; the test of the correctness of a radical critique is its ability to bring genuine human problems suffered by men to a "self-conscious human form." For Max Horkheimer, in *Critical Theory*,[4] "It is the task of critical theory to see 'the human bottom of nonhuman things' and to demystify the surface forms of equality." This *can* be a function of radical criticism and it is this function which the authors of this volume seek to fulfill.

[4] Max Horkheimer. *Critical Theory: Selected Essays.* Matthew J. O'Connell, translator. New York: Herder & Herder, Inc., 1972.

Section II
CRITICISM

OUR CRITICISM OF SCHOOLING deals in some depth only with those phenomena of schooling that are of special concern to one (or more) of us, six authors in search of meaning. Our common focus is the attempt to deal with the fundamental questions about schooling in our historical context. We have grappled with this task over a three year period, in an effort to sharpen our collective critical consciousness. The questions that shape our common effort are the following:

1. How are human relationships influenced by social institutions; by schooling in particular?

2. Does education have a unique or major function in society? What is that role? What are the given meanings of schooling in our historical context?

3. How do those meanings serve the interests of specific groups while maintaining the powerlessness and dependency of other groups?

4. What are the mechanisms of domination through schooling?

5. What contradictions do we see in the way schools presently operate that reflect discrepancies between our humane ideals and our political practices and that constitute a false consciousness?

6. What structures in society embody and perpetuate that false consciousness?

7. How can we move from the question of "who is messing up the schools" to the question of "whose interests are served by schooling"?

8. What tools and modes does the educator need to penetrate and illuminate the false consciousness, to "demystify the surface forms of equality," to disclose the political realities of schooling?

9. How can we help educators to see that the systematic politicization of schools is part of the larger political effort of society to maintain the status quo?

10. Where do educators look for partnerships and alliances in the common task of restructuring society and schooling on a more just and equitable basis?

11. Should schools be criticized as though they were the spearheads of changes that have not taken place in society?

12. What is the nature and function of education that is liberating rather than dominating?

What follows are six presentations that grew out of our collective analyses and individual interpretations of these questions.

1. The Contradiction Between the Recreative and the Established

Dwayne Huebner

AT ONE TIME many of us chose to be educators. In my case, the choice grew out of dissatisfaction with my own education. I looked about and saw that my life was not as satisfying as I thought it could be. I presumed that the quality of my education had something to do with the discrepancy between what I seemed to be and what I felt were my possibilities. When a second vocational choice point arrived I decided to be a teacher. Four years later, two years in preparation and two years as a school teacher, I still did not know how to reduce the gap between actuality and possibility. My teaching colleagues and I still seemed unable to close the discrepancy between what we thought our students might be and what they were able to do in school. Today, the conditions which influenced my decision to be an educator may no longer hold. Perhaps I continue to be an educator because I have been one for a long time—it is now the path of least resistance and it provides a reasonable living style.

Reflecting upon my original choice to be an educator, I am certain that I had in mind, perhaps vaguely, the intention to help individuals be more self-fulfilling, more powerful, more capable of recognizing and realizing their own possibilities as human beings. After all, that is what I wanted for myself. That I chose to be a teacher in a school implied at that time that I saw no easier way to help individuals be educated. I assumed that learning to teach in a school would enable me to help individuals realize more fully and more powerfully their own possibilities.

I soon discovered that helping an individual realize his or her own possibilities sometimes came in conflict with maintaining the order and routines of a classroom and school. The fact that I had to fulfill my intention of being an educator by being a school functionary did not strike me as being unrealistic. The distinction between being an educator and being a school teacher was not transparent to me at that time, nor to most educators. Today it is.

I am certain that my decision to be a teacher never entailed being a functionary in school. The school was simply a place to be an educator. In those early years, I neither questioned the existence of the school nor gave it primary allegiance. I presumed that education, in part, took place there and I saw my possibility as an educator to exist in school and school related institutions. That I could not realize my image to be an educator within schools meant that my colleagues and I needed better skills or that schools had to be improved. Never did it mean that schools had to be abolished. Today I can see more clearly the school as a historical institution in which educational functions have been confused with noneducational functions. Whether the school can ever be an institution devoted solely to education now seems problematical.

I still would not choose to be simply a functionary in a school today. I would not choose to maintain a school or permit maintenance functions to overcome or take precedence over education. To the extent that education can occur within a school I was and am willing to manifest my vocation as an educator throughout the school. To the extent that the maintenance of schools interferes with educating young people, I would as soon see schools change, evolve into something else, or wither away and be replaced by other educational formats. As the educational limitations of the school become more obvious, I am now willing to help people be educators no matter what their institutional commitments or lack of them.

The Bureaucracy vs. the People

The tension between educating the individual and maintaining an orderly classroom and school resides not in the school as a bureaucratic institution with defined expectancies and roles. Behind the roles and the expectancies, behind the bureaucracy and the orderliness, are the interests of people. People have invested their lives and their meanings in the school, its maintenance, and its supporting mechanisms and ideologies. The tension made manifest in the conflict between the possible education of the individual and the maintenance of the school is the tension between those who have an interest in a future emerging in the lives of the children and young people, and those who have a future which now exists in their everydayness—the structures, orderliness, and meanings attached to the school and school related pursuits.

The tension between young people and their potential future and adults and their future, manifest in their everydayness, provokes the intent to control one individual by other individuals. Given the lingo that we educators use, control is hidden and justified behind such terms as learning, socialization, citizenship, and responsibility. Politically, such control would be spoken of as social control, oppression, or domination. However we label it, the tension is a consequence of the struggle between the new and the old, between re-creation and preservation or conservation.

Given my original choice to help young people live out and realize their own possibilities through education, how did I live in this tension between the young person's own future, or at least his or her rightful claim on that future, and the already established present of others, mine included, and our presumed right to maintain that present as a future for ourselves and perhaps for our students? How did I live in the presence of those of us who seek to dominate others, those of us who seek to escape domination and perhaps by way of excess, end up dominating others? I denied the existence of the tension. The conflict between the established and the emergent was seen as an educational problem. As a problem, the tension could be removed if the problem could be solved. It could be a problem of the aims of education, to be solved by an adequate educational philosophy and a more profound statement of the purposes and functions of education in a "democracy." It could be a problem of teaching method, to be solved by better scientific study of teaching and other strategies of teaching and instruction. It could be a problem of the management and change of educational institutions and solved by better management procedures or educational change strategies.

Given the doctrine of progress which dominates schooling and school people, I lived in the tension challenged by problems that could be defined rationally and solved methodologically. Whereas the rational definition of problems and the methodological solution of them is usually interpreted as an interest-free and objective procedure, it in effect established a new manifestation of the tension between the new, the recreative, and the old, the already established.

Seeing a conflict in interest as a problem which can succumb to proper methodologies leads to the establishment of a new interest group—the academic specialist of education who takes on and "solves" so-called educational problems. The interests of the academic educational specialist are the interests of school people who seek to overcome or hide the tensions between the emergent, the young, and the already established, and the interests of the academic community which seeks to maintain a purity of method and a presumed objectivity of knowledge. Schooling problems are to be defined in terms of existing academic or scholarly canons and the methods employed must conform to the methodologies which have been shown by the academic community to be free of "bias" or "error." The academically based educator, while proclaiming the possibilities of young people, at the same time affirms the production of knowledge which is a response to the questions and problems of the institutional practitioner of education. This knowledge production can be research—the development of more warranted theories; it can be technology—the development of methods or materials which embody warranted knowledge; or it can be training—the preparation of functionaries who will, through their advanced skills, be able to alleviate the tensions sensed by others.

The academically based educator's interest in the problems of educational functionaries is complicated by his or her interest in membership in the academic community and its rightful concern for the maintenance of purity of method and objectivity of knowledge. Neither the problems which concern the educator in his or her knowledge production, and the technologizing of that knowledge in method, materials, or skill; nor the concern for purity of method or objectivity of results necessarily coincides with the interests of the young in their own possibilities, unless the young choose to take on the interest of the academic.

The Possibilities of the Young

My decision to be a teacher—to be committed to helping other individuals realize their possibilities—did not entail a conscious decision to take on problems posed by functionaries nor to take on the norms guiding academic work. Nevertheless, I have tacitly chosen to be an academic. Many of us have. In so doing, we have permitted the norms and concerns of academia to take precedence over our concern for the possibilities of individual young people. In rejecting the role of institutional functionary, which seemed to conflict with educating the young, we have taken on another role which conflicts in other ways with their possibilities. The tension made manifest in the conflict between the realization of the possibilities of youth through education and the maintenance of our role as academically based educator is also a tension between those who have an interest in a future emerging in the lives of children and young people, and those of us who have a future in our everydayness —in this case the priorities and norms of academia: purity of method, objectivity of knowledge, and solution of social problems.

Does our interest in knowledge production, and the rituals that accompany it, provide a source of conflict with the young, and lead us into forms of social control, oppression, and domination? Do our knowledge systems which presumably explain the growth and development of young people, the mechanisms of socialization, and the processes of learning serve as oppressive symbolic systems which demand that the young interpret their experience by our experience? Is our purity of method and objectivity used to deny the absolute uniqueness of each young person? Is our search for scientific understanding an effort to categorize the young so we need not assume personal responsibility for being with them in a complicated drama of mutual influence?

Today I recognize that the tension between young people and educators—whether functionaries in schools or functionaries in academia—is not a symptom of a problem. The tension between the new, manifest in the lives of the young, and the old, manifest in the already established, is a basic human tension. It exists because men, women, and children do not have a nature. They have only a past and a future which collide in the present. The consequences of that collision are limited by the way power is distributed, exercised in human relationships, and controlled by custom and law.

Today, then, I have to stand in this tension between the new and the old, the future and the past, aware of the weak and the strong, of the powerless and the powerful. I must stand aware of the need for a just distribution of power so the outcome of the tension cannot be predicted but can be judged fair and equitable. No longer can the welfare of the weak or the powerless be left to chance, often whimsical; nor to the benevolence of the powerful, often guilt-laden; nor to the love by the more experienced, often distorted by self-interest.

Somehow the weak and the powerless, the young, who must be protected by the adult from potential danger and destruction, must also be protected from the unjust control of the strong and the powerful—the very adult who claims to be the protector. The young are not protected by educational philosophies or by predefined objectives and evaluation measures. These rhetorics of the educator are legitimations for their power or slogans which offer no protection against misuses or abuses of power. The unjust domination of the young can be restricted only by the conscious concern for the equal and/or just distribution of power. This can be accomplished through moral consideration, but is primarily accomplished through legal consideration. Somehow, then, my professed interests in the future of young people in the realization of their own possibilities, must be embodied in the struggle to assure the rights of the young against the unjust domination of those in power.

For educators, this tension between the new and the old, the recreative and the already established, has special significance, for ostensibly our primary concerns are with the future. The school based educator faces this tension in the conflict between the young and the institutional necessities and regularities. The academically based educator faces this tension in the conflicts over the articulation, interpretation, and explanation of the functionings of the human world.

Collisions Between the Future and the Past

In institutional settings the consequences of the collisions between the future and the past, or the past as present, are controlled by the structures of governance. The governance structure distributes and sanctions power. The formal and informal relationships are the embodiment of this power. The customs of judgment and discipline, the quasi-legal procedures of the institution, adjudicate conflict. When conflict within the school becomes visible and of concern to those who are outside the school, then individuals or groups with political power can employ the legal structures of the society—the administrative, legislative, and judicial processes of government— to adjudicate and govern within the school. This is now happening in the student and teacher rights movements and in community control efforts.

The continuing expansion of constitutional rights to young people in schools and to teachers and other educators will facilitate the more equitable distribution and use of power. When the legal and constitutional constraints on the misuses of power find their way into the school, then we educators can live more comfortably in this tension between the young and their future and the adults and their institutions. In a collision of interests governed by law, we need to be less guilty of our presumed benevolence and less neurotic about our presumed love.

Under just laws which cover the schools and the formal relationships within the schools, the inviolability of the young can be protected from my self-interest and the self-interest of other educators. The tension between the young and the old is not a symptom of a problem to be solved. It is a necessary rift in our social fabric which must be maintained, by law, if our institutions are to evolve and to provide new forms in which all can live together justly.

To profess an interest in the possibilities of young people entails involvement in the struggle to extend constitutional rights to the young, to establish mechanisms by which the quasi-legal structure of our educational institutions corresponds to the legal structure of the society at large, and to evolve ways in which the young actively participate in the continual shaping and reshaping of those institutions within which they dwell as students. To profess an interest in the possibilities by being only a teacher or curriculum worker in the more or less traditional sense is to encourage our own interests, shaped in the past, manifest in the present, and determining of our future, to take precedence over the interest of the young. To profess an interest in the future of young people is to seek to increase their power in order to make more equitable the distribution of power in the struggle between the past and the future.

In the academic setting and in the diverse realms of knowledge, with their differing methods and standards of warranty or truthfulness, the tension between the new and the old, the recreative and the already established, is controlled or monitored with greater difficulty. The academically based educator, with an interest in purity of method and objectivity of knowledge, easily and naturally imposes his or her own interpretations and explanations of the functionings of the human world upon the young. Our expertise and knowledge become unwitting vehicles for the exercise of power over the young and the formation of the young. The distribution of power seems inequitable in this tension between the young and the adult as they interpret, make sense of, and explain the functionings of the human world.

The adults' interpretations of events and people are readily seen as truth and absolutized. There is no ready recourse to law to moderate or adjudicate between the conflicts, as there is in conflicts centered in institutional or social life. The movement toward the democratization of institutional life can be seen in the extension of constitutional rights to women and the young. The democratization of knowledge seems like a foreign and perhaps destructive notion, which will lead to a downgrading of standards and a potential adverse effect on our ways of life which are influenced or determined by that knowledge production of academia or other men and women of knowledge.

The Possibilities Within the School

In the midst of this tension I am unsure and know not how to proceed with any confidence. How does a concern for the just distribution of power apply to knowledge production and utilization? Perhaps part of the resolution will be found in the extension of our constitutional ideas of freedom of speech to education. If we have the political right to freely express our ideas and commitments, does not this right extend to the young in classrooms and schools? How do our unquestioned procedures of evaluation and grading infringe on this right? Certainly today there is sufficient reason to associate speech with knowledge, and to make the claim that to know is manifest in our ability to speak or to act. The control and domination of conversation in classrooms by teachers, by institutional necessities and regularities, and by limited educational material can be interpreted as a restriction on the freedom of speech.

Part of the resolution of this conflict will be found in greater attention by the educator to the traditions associated with the sociology of knowledge, and the way in which consciousness and false consciousness are shaped by prevailing social patterns. Part of the resolution will be found in the existing traditions of dialog as a form of human relationship and the increased concern for hermeneutics, the art of interpretation. Part of the resolution will be found as we increasingly recognize that the positivistic studies of the young, whether human development and psychology or socialization and sociology, often intrude on our responsiveness to the young as carriers of criticisms, novelty, and newness. Increased concern for the history of childhood and youth will eventually provide greater awareness of the adult's relationship with the young.

To profess an interest in the possibilities of the young entails, then, great doubt about our forms of commerce in knowledge and our ways of warranting and judging truth. It entails greater attention to listening as a way of being with others and as a way of making judgments about the validity and usefulness of our accepted forms of knowledge, speech, and action. It entails greater attention to the structures of institutions and the structures of interpersonal situations which restrict freedom of speech and movement of all people. It entails accepting doubt as a primary factor or element in all forms of knowing and action.

The intention behind my original choice was to help individual children be more self-fulfilling, more powerful, more capable of recognizing and realizing their own possibilities as human beings. I assumed that the possibilities of the young were native to them, and that the school merely developed these possibilities. The 60's destroyed that illusion. The so-called disadvantaged are not genetically disadvantaged. They are disadvantaged because human possibility is not fairly nor even randomly distributed. In learning to teach in school, I learned to educate those who found that the possibilities distributed in school were indeed their possibilities. For those who did not recognize their possibilities in the school I learned to "motivate," to "build readiness," to "direct attention." As a group, educators learned to provide "head starts" so more children could find their possibilities in the possibilities already established in schools.

To motivate, to build readiness, to direct attention, to give head starts, are not necessarily educational activities in the sense of helping children to be more self-fulfilling, more powerful, more capable of recognizing and realizing their own possibilities. These activities are more often than not alienating activities which seek to pull children away from their own possibilities and to impose the possibilities of others upon them. Instead of self-fulfilling, these activities can make them fulfilling of others; instead of developing potency, these activities can be developing impotency; instead of recognizing their own possibilities they can be recognizing the possibilities of others which can never be their own. For many children the possibilities within the school were not their possibilities.

In learning to teach in schools, then, I learned how to operate within my possibilities, for I obviously taught in schools with those who shared my sense of the possible. My failure to be successful with all young pupils and my failure to be able to speak helpfully to and with those who were committed to educating children with different possibilities, pointed not to a lack of educational skill on my part. It pointed to a lack of awareness of the pluralities of human possibilities, and to lack of understanding of how these possibilities are indeed carried by existing institutions and modes of social life.

In attempting to educate an individual child, not only did I come up against a tension between the future of that child and the meaning structure of the school; I also came up against a void within the school and within myself. Given my original choice to help young people realize and live out their own possibilities through education, how do I stand in this void separating the possibilities existing in school from the possibilities in the child which cannot be realized in the school? In the past, I stood there as if this were an educational problem. How can I motivate the child to accept the possibilities that are carried by the school? How can I make modifications in the curriculum so it will have some relevance for the child? I did not deny the existence of the void; but it was a void within the educational world and could be filled by educationists with more of the same merely extended to the newfound emptiness.

A Gap in the Public World

Today I recognize the void for what it is—a gap in the public world which extends far beyond the school. This does not mean that I know how to fill it. Perhaps I can ask different questions about its existence as a void and how the public world must be changed to fill in the void, or perhaps to distribute the void more equitably. It is a problem for which I have only the beginning forms of the questions and none of the answers. The questions pertain to how our possibilities for ourselves and for others are made accessible to each and every person on this small earth. In part, it is a question of technology and the many ways in which human possibility is preserved, communicated, taken on.

Possibility is obviously carried by the institutions of production, exchange, and consumption. Possibility is marketed via jobs and professions and the schools which tie into these jobs and professions. Possibility is marketed in terms of recreation, travel, and goods. Possibility is displayed in the commercial media via advertisements and the styles of life embodied in public works of art and non-art, in film, TV, and print. Possibility is carried by the materials and methods used in schools—the stories in arithmetic books, the interpretations of human life in the social studies, the visions of a "more perfect thing" world in the science materials, the way we are as we are educated with others.

But the distribution of possibility is also a matter of power and control, and consequently, law. Possibility does not reside within the neurological structure of the individual. It exists at the boundary between the individual and the life styles that have been forged by all our predecessors and left in the tools, images, habits, institutions, memories, and visions embodied in the public world. This is the public wealth—just as the resources of the earth are public wealth, even though controlled by limited interest groups. Why should this wealth be distributed only to those who purchase it, or have inherited it, or have power over it? Why should the wealth of the literary traditions be reserved to those who speak only one style of English? Why should the tools for social analysis and criticism be available only to those who wish to maintain the present social-economic structure? Why should the diverse traditions associated with the Orient or Africa be available only to those within those traditions or to those who can afford the luxury of travel or who have the skills or scholarship?

Thus the distribution of possibility is influenced by the structures of justice that mediate the distribution of wealth among people in this world. The possibilities available to the young and the possibilities withheld from them, whether in the home or the school or in other institutions of the society, can also come under the control of law.

Finally, possibility is also carried by the intentions and the memories of various social groups. Communism is not carried by capitalists; Buddhism is not carried by Christians; certain life styles are not carried by the poor; certain negations of the present and images of the future are not carried by the rich. Hence accessibility to certain possibilities means access to certain social groups and their memories, disciplines, and intentions. If children are removed from the community within which they dwell and placed into the memories, intentions, and life styles of other communities, then they may also be pulled away from their own possibilities and into those of others.

How do I stand, then, on the edge of the void separating me and my possibilities as they are given in the school, from the possibilities of the young? Today, I must stand there aware of how children come up against possibility, recognize it as such, and accept it or reject it as their possibility. This requires awareness that the concern for the possibilities of the individual without equal concern for the social-political-economic conditions within which we all live is hollow and meaningless.

2. Women/Schooling/Society

Esther Zaret

IN WOMAN'S STRUGGLE FOR EQUALITY, in the individual and collective search for meaning, schooling continues to be an obstructive and repressive force. Schools do not in themselves create the oppression of women, nor can they in themselves end it. Yet as the institution charged with responsibility for maintaining the social, economic, and political status quo in society, schooling has the decisive functions of inducting girls and boys into a priori roles of dominated and dominant, then rationalizing those roles through an elaborate system of myths, real life modeling, and skewed opportunities for fulfillment in adult life.

Schools are not only not in search of meanings but if successful they block the search. Schools *are* a set of meanings, but only those meanings that preserve the status quo, perpetuating the "realities" of the social order as perceived, structured, and defended by the dominant group. Among those realities is a lifetime of disequilibrium between woman and man.

As a woman and an educator I am particularly concerned with exposing the bases and mechanisms for the domination of women through schooling, and searching, with others, for educational forms and directions that can be a liberating force for women as well as for other oppressed groups.

My essay touches on four facets of the problem: women's new consciousness and the old realities; the school as a repressive force in women's lives; the role of the feminist educator as an agent of transition; and, a conception of education as liberating rather than dominating.

The New Consciousness and the Old Realities

Women, in increasing numbers, *are* awakening to the consciousness of their oppression as a class in our society. Women *are* articulating, in sudden numbers and with stunning clarity, a manifesto of
grievances documenting their oppression and their individual and
collective paths to a new consciousness. Yet this new consciousness
is uneven and fragile. Many of the dramatic changes taking place in
women's lives during the past few years seem more appropriately
related to the aspirations and methods of the feminist movements
of the 20's and 30's than those of the 70's.

The movement of the 70's, dubbed the "Second Feminist Wave"
by the *New York Times*, differs radically from the feminist movement
of the 20's in its emphasis on analyzing and changing the economic
and social bases of women's continuing oppression as a class. The
feminist movement of the 20's and 30's was not concerned with the
political realities of sexism. With its roots in 19th century feminism,
it was concerned with providing a class of privileged women with
equal access to a male dominated world, not with understanding or
changing the structural bases of women's oppression. In its failure
to transcend the suffrage issue with a more radical analysis of the
structural causes of women's oppression, the earlier feminist movement culminated in the search for private-personal solutions to the
denial of full equality for women.

It is apparent today that many women are still seeking and
finding private-personal solutions to self-fulfillment within the framework of our sexist society. Women are achieving in sports, politics,
and space exploration. Women are on active duty in police depart-
ments; women in unprecedented numbers are entering professional
schools of medicine, law, engineering, and architecture. In many
smaller cities women are mayors; in many states women hold state
and federal elective posts and, perhaps as a temporary culmination
of such progress, in Connecticut the first woman ever elected in
her own right to the governorship of any state has recently taken
office. We have witnessed a serious attempt to nominate a woman
for the Presidency of the United States; the Equal Rights Amendment prohibiting any form of sex discrimination by any government, local, state, or federal, has been ratified in 33 states (and
only two states have rescinded their votes although the National
Women's Political Caucus believes that the possibility of attempts
to rescind earlier ratification is rather widespread).

And in June 1974, the U.S. Department of Health, Education, and Welfare published proposed regulations for ending sex discrimination in education. According to their reports they would ban such common discriminatory school practices as offering home economics courses solely to girls and shop courses solely to boys. The proposed regulations would also require fundamental changes in athletic programs, recruitment and admission policies in graduate and professional schools that receive federal aid, the abolishment of quotas, and also prohibit discrimination "on the basis of pregnancy and related conditions." Significantly, the greatest controversy during the preparation of the rules involved the field of athletics (man's last bastion?). Even more significant was the complete omission from the regulations of one of the most widely acknowledged areas of sexism in schooling—the question of discriminatory curriculum materials, such as textbooks that contain sex bias.

The New Feminine Consciousness

Do these changes signal progress? A social revolution? In the new feminine consciousness they are recognized as ameliorative measures, the reluctant response of the system to unprecedented and accumulating social pressures of feminist groups. Neither the personal-private solution nor ameliorative measures, such as those proposed by the U.S. Department of Health, Education, and Welfare, attempt to deal with, nor do they acknowledge, the structural bases for the continued domination of women. In the political realities of sexism neither "equal educational opportunities" nor "equal access" will mean more than token "equality," for some privileged women.

Perhaps the most crucial aspect of the new consciousness is the understanding of these realities and the profound change in women's attitudes toward themselves. Private-personal solutions are gradually giving way to a collective consciousness and collective action that articulate women's goals clearly and mobilize group resources more effectively. What women are saying is that we want full and equal stature as full and equal human beings. We want, as stated by Simone de Beauvoir, that *all* of us, not some of us, will never have to "sense in our femininity an inconvenience or an obstacle." We want to explore the myths and reconstruct, step by step, the historical bases for the emergence of women as an oppressed class; we want to disclose the dialectic of our oppression and the nature of the society we live in; we want the outrage, the indignity, the oppressive reality of sexism to become an intimate facet of the *public* as well as the *personal* consciousness. And we want our schooling restructured to help us uncover the myths, disclose the realities, and create the conditions in which girls and boys, women and men can engage in cooperative reflection and action for transforming the objective conditions of the society we live in.

The School as a Repressive Force

In the present structure of society women are a dominated and powerless group despite an impressive record of individual achievements. As a class women share the distinctive and demeaning characteristics of other oppressed groups:

- Acceptance of their traditional and inferior status as somehow natural and right
- Falsification or omission from history of their unique past, their special achievements, their distinctive present
- Limitations in their access to status and leadership roles in economic, academic, and political spheres
- Economic dependency on the dominant class
- Token recognition and limited acceptance of the token few who make it
- Lack of a collective consciousness of oppression
- Lack of a collective effort to change the status of the group
- The search for private-personal solutions rather than identifying and eliminating the social bases of oppression.

The structures and mechanisms of social domination are subtle, pervasive, and universally accepted. Our educational system is exquisitely designed to maintain the status quo by affirming existing structural relationships among power groups and dependent-dominated groups and perpetuating myths that are the legitimating basis for those relationships. Schooling thus has a specialized role in maintaining the domination of women. Some of the structures and mechanisms of that domination have been disclosed and carefully documented in the women's movement of the 60's and 70's.

The most blatant expressions are overt practices such as these:

- Differences in teacher expectations for girls and boys (and women and men)
- Sexism in textbooks, instructional materials, methods, and content of instruction

• Role modeling on all educational levels where a disproportionate number of teachers are women, while administrators and other (higher) authorities are men

• "Guiding" women away from "masculine" professions such as engineering, medicine, law, aviation, architecture

• Lower salaries and lower ratio of achievement of rank and tenure in higher education for women in the same positions and with at least the same qualifications as men

• Discrepancy in numbers of women and men in all higher education positions, particularly in administration.

These practices preclude or deny a woman's consciousness of her oppression by subtly limiting the definitions of her possibilities for becoming. Simone de Beauvoir stresses the validity of defining woman (as man) in a human rather than a mechanistic perspective; as a being who is not fixed:

Woman is not a completed reality, but rather a becoming, and it is in her becoming that . . . her *possibilities* should be defined. . . . for the fact is that capabilities are clearly manifested only when they have been realized—but the fact is also that when we have to do with a being whose nature is transcendent action, we can never close the books.[1]

Schools not only "close the books" prematurely on woman's becoming, they use sex biased books that circumscribe the girl-woman's consciousness of her own possibilities for self-fulfillment. These overt manifestations of sexism in schooling have been criticized, documented, and in many instances modified by the pressures of feminists together with concerned parent groups, educators, and students. The more elusive phenomena of oppression, highly resistant to scrutiny and change, are those themes, practices, and basic school-society structures that sustain the popularized myths and stereotypes of female-male relationships; it is these phenomena that reveal the essential class bias of schooling.

Woman's oppression is grounded in the nature of the society we live in. Not only education but our entire society "domesticizes" women to adopt their traditional and inferior roles. The dynamics of the socialization process (Freire calls it domesticization) are played out through schooling in overt practices such as those mentioned earlier but also through more pervasive and subtle modes: the introjection of popularized myths; the omission from history of

[1] Simone de Beauvoir. *The Second Sex.* H. M. Parshley, translator and editor. New York: Alfred A. Knopf, Inc., 1952. p. 30.

salient information; the affirmation of social structures that perpetuate the power balance of dominated and dominant groups.

A crucial force in sustaining the structural relationships of dependency and power between woman and man is the myth of woman's status as innately dependent, biologically determined, and necessarily relating to the world through male mediation. Schooling affirms this notion through practices and structures such as these:

Raising the question of woman's capabilities in comparison to men

Rewarding woman's acceptance of masculine values and her own inequality

Isolating women from establishing bonds with other women; emphasizing, instead, competition for male approval

Subverting woman's access to higher education and "masculine" fields of study

Providing role models in which women teachers become, in turn, instruments for maintaining the myths of woman's inferiority.

In attempting to disclose reality, to displace self-serving myths of an inherent inequality of the sexes, feminist writers are emphasizing the need for "theoretical differentiation between the symptoms and the causes" of women's oppression.[2] Schooling promotes the symptoms and avoids the issue of "causes." In the feminist view the second class status of women is a social-economic-political phenomenon of civilized society. Women were not always and not everywhere subordinate; the reversal in women's status coincided with fundamental changes in the structure of society: the advent of private property, class society, and monogamous marriage. Schooling avoids the issue of "causes" by omitting, de-emphasizing, or distorting information relevant to the history of women's domination. Examples of missing highlights:

A full accounting of contributions of women to social progress, the role individual women have played in the history of the human race [3]

[2] Friedrich Engels. In: Eleanor Burke Leacock, editor. *The Origin of the Family, Private Property, and the State*. New York: International Publishers, 1972. pp. 45-46, in Introduction by Leacock.

[3] Betty Roszak. "The Human Continuum." In: Betty Roszak and Theodore Roszak, editors. *Masculine/Feminine: Readings in Sexual Mythology and the Liberation of Women*. New York: Harper & Row, Publishers, 1969. p. 302.

The history of women's movements of the past (and the present)

Studies of women's status and roles in pre-civilization societies

Investigations of the change from matrilineality ("mother right" of descent) that historically preceded patrilineality ("father right")

Engels' argument "that the position of women relative to men deteriorated with the advent of private property and class society"; and, "the first class oppression coincides with that of the female sex by the male" [4]

Attention to "ethnographic and historical data (supportive of Engels' theory) showing that women's social position has not always, everywhere, or in most respects been subordinate to that of men." [5]

If these basic concepts have been de-emphasized in schooling they have, with great effort, been incorporated in the new feminist consciousness. Questioning the realities of oppressive social institutions, from marriage to the nuclear family to schooling, women have collectively probed to deeper levels of consciousness in what Firestone calls "a careful joint observation, to resensitize a fractured consciousness." [6]

One of the most frustrating anomalies to be disclosed is the contradiction in which women, just as other exploited groups, are "dependent upon structures that oppose their own interests, (and are thus) compelled to act against themselves." The dilemma is particularly acute for women who are educators. Françoise Giroud, the new French Secretary of State for the Condition of Women, sharpens the issue in her recent statement:

Every woman is two persons: one, part of the fabric of society, who may variously want to conserve it intact, change it, or destroy it; the other, who must confront a special situation—being a woman. [7]

Each woman educator must recognize that within its own substructure the educational establishment replicates the societal power relationships in a parallel (but subordinate) hierarchy of its own

[4] Engels, *op. cit.*, p. 129.

[5] Karen Sacks. "Engels Revisited: Women, The Organization of Production and Private Property." In: Michelle Zimbalist Rosaldo and Louise Lamphere, editors. *Women, Culture, and Society.* Stanford, California: Stanford University Press, 1974. p. 207.

[6] Shulamith Firestone. *The Dialectic of Sex: The Case for Feminist Revolution.* New York: Bantam Books, Inc., 1971. pp. 1-2.

[7] Françoise Giroud. "Allons Personnes de la Patrie . . ." In: *The New York Times,* August 26, 1974. Adapted from *L'Express,* translated by Leonard Mayhew. © 1974 by The New York Times Company. Reprinted by permission.

power groups, each with its own interests in controlling decision-making processes. Do you wish to conserve the power relationships intact? change them? destroy them? Each woman educator must also consider a moral issue: If schooling is manipulative and oppressive, am I as a woman and an educator a complicitor in that domination? Am I as an administrator an oppressor by definition? According to Freire, power elites within dependent groups tend to dominate their own people. Am I, then, caught in the friction of the private-personal solution at the cost of the collective effort? For me, the answer is "yes"; by participating in the rewards of a repressive form of schooling, I am an agent of that system. Reflected in my position is a tacit acceptance of a change in my status from the dominated to the dominant class. For me, however, the answer also points to a special opportunity and responsibility for acting as an agent of transition to a liberating form of schooling.

I believe that women as educators are in a unique position to sharpen public consciousness of the social bases for domination of women in schooling and to act as agents of transition to new educational forms and practices.

The Teacher as Transition Agent

The woman educator who decides that her stake in schooling (and society) is to change it has two functions: she can work with others in developing collectively a vision (model) of what schooling for liberation should be; she can be a catalyst in detonating a "new conflict zone," an opening in which, as Huebner puts it, "social novelty might erupt." Habermas has concluded that neither the old class antagonisms nor the new type of underprivilege contains a protest potential . . . gravitating toward a new conflict zone.[8] I believe that the accelerating feminist movement, in concert with the efforts of other oppressed groups, has the power to generate and detonate a new conflict zone in society. The process has already begun.

An immediate task for women who are educators is to articulate their individual paths from domination—to dominance—to liberation. The task is parallel to that of feminists who individually and collectively are articulating a new consciousness of their social domination. The task embraces three phases of a groping development: *Articulation; Awareness; Affiliation.*

[8] Jürgen Habermas. *Toward a Rational Society.* London: Heineman Educational Books, Ltd., 1971.

Articulation of woman's objective conditions means the disclosure of personal meanings, a sharing of the experiences, the special joys, the pain, the contradictions of growing up female in a male dominant society. The woman who is an educator has a double commitment in piercing the veil of myths and meanings that have surrounded her schooling and growth, to disclose for herself as well as others the import and impact of the given meanings.

In my personal struggle for meanings, school was a detracting force echoing and rewarding my docile compliance in the put-down of my femininity and special personhood, granting recognition and rewards for a surface display of "intelligence," existing apart from my real learning at home, through books, and in real life together with real people. School and learning were always distinctly separate for me. Because of recurring economic flip-flops we moved, very often. I attended five elementary schools and three high schools. In all schools I was a good student; that is, I learned quickly what it was "they" wanted and I did learn how to please.

I was not only a good student, I was a "good girl," too. As an only daughter among four sons I was appreciated, applauded, fussed over, indulged—and exploited. In a male dominant household (not only in numbers, but in force of personality) I was retarded in asserting my femininity as a positive force in my own development, in the lives of my family, and in my teaching.

I was a grown woman with two children in school before I learned the excitement, the frustrations, and the satisfactions of real learning—dealing honestly and thoroughly with problems that have meaning for me. It was then, too, that I began to question the contradiction of considering myself a liberated woman in a society in which women are a dominated class.

It is through sharing with others the continuing contradictions of my life as a woman and educator that I have come to know that these contradictions are not personal-petty; they reflect accurately contradictions embodied in the class structure of our society.

Awareness evolves on two levels: subjective awareness of contradictions inherent in the roles of woman as educator; and, awareness of contradictions and ambiguities in the objective conditions of society. Every woman educator faces a network of contradictions inherent in her dual roles as woman and as educator. Initially each of us must resolve the paradox of conformity. Schools are places where conformity is valued; educators are "educated" to conform. How do we break out of that mode to provide leadership for others? *Contradiction:* The woman educator has a stake in maintaining a repressive structure that opposes her interests as a woman. Women educators are in a very real sense acting against themselves; we are "complicitors in our own domination."[9] *Contradiction:* Women educators simultaneously occupy antithetical positions of power and powerlessness. As educators we are the dominant class, the power elite within the substructure of the school; as women we are the dominated class in schools as in society. *Contradiction:* The latent discrepancy between a woman's original motive in becoming an educator versus the current reality and extent of her professional commitment. Was the original choice a matter of easier job access for women? A response to societal expectations and stereotypes that assign nurturing-tenderness functions to women? *Contradiction:* The bureaucratic structures of schooling remove educators from the immediate jurisdiction of the public while stressing public "accountability." This disparity blocks the full development of a personal and professional sense of responsibility and accomplishment. *Contradiction:* The conflicting orientations (and pressures) of pursuing a career to the fullest in the face of the stereotype that equates ambition with unladylike aggression.[10] Many of these contradictions in a woman educator's life are definitely self-contradictory.

There can be no resolution of the exposed contradictions until these insights are expressed in some form of constructive action in one's immediate context. For women who are teachers the starting point is *you* in *your* own *situation.* Examine your place in your institution: are you the dominant or dominated; do you define your interests with either of these groups; is that where you want to be? Help your students to recognize and challenge the stereotypes about women (and men), about other oppressed groups. Take leadership in developing the notion that schools belong *to the people.* Examine the power structure in your institution: who makes decisions; in whose interests are those decisions made? Work with students and other teachers in critical analysis of texts, materials, methods, and content of instruction. Examine suggested ameliorative

---

[9] A forceful phrase and conception used by Barbara Harrison in: *Unlearning the Lie: Sexism in School.* New York: William Morrow and Co., Inc., 1974. I believe it is even more apt in pinpointing the essence of the woman educator's dilemma.

[10] Elizabeth Koontz. *The Best Kept Secret of the Past 5,000 Years: Women Are Ready for Leadership in Education.* Bloomington, Indiana: The Phi Delta Kappa Educational Foundation, 1972. p. 46.

measures: are they basic changes or superficial measures designed to silence criticism and maintain the status quo?

These are the areas of the teacher's unexamined realities. Examining and acting on these realities creates the conditions for *affiliation*, the process of transcending the personal-immediate situation for collective reflection and action in a broader social context. In ASCD, for example, there are a number of caucuses representing the interests of various minority and oppressed groups: Women's Caucus; Black Caucus; American Indian Caucus; Radical Caucus, etc.

In another dimension of affiliation women scholars are combining efforts to probe old assumptions and stereotypes, to challenge the prevailing ideology that controls women's lives, and to produce new insights—new meanings—for and about women in every aspect of their daily lives. There are examples of such cooperative works in every scholarly field. An outstanding contribution is a collection of essays edited by Rosaldo and Lamphere that "illustrate ways in which anthropologists will have to begin to think about women if they are to understand our human world." According to the authors, "these papers represent a first generation's attempt to integrate an interest in women into a general theory of society and culture." [11]

Throughout the country, women educators, students on every educational level, and grass-roots community women are participating in the critical analysis of the culture that shaped them and keeps them in their place.

In such cooperative, critical efforts the collective consciousness is developed and refined; the unity of individual interests with the interests of other women, other oppressed groups, is clarified and understood. The process is ultimately a political effort because it must deal with the relationships of powerless and power groups in schooling and in society. Collective efforts in developing a critical analysis of the objective conditions of society are both a necessary precondition and a model for a liberating education.

Schooling as a Liberating Force [12]

My view of the nature and function of schooling that is liberating rather than dominating embraces two fundamental processes:

[11] Rosaldo and Lamphere, *op. cit.*, pp. vi, 15.

[12] My view of schooling as a liberating force is an incomplete conception at this time. It leans heavily on Freire's work (particularly, "Cultural Action for Freedom"). See also James B. Macdonald, Bernice J. Wolfson, and Esther Zaret. *Reschooling Society: A Conceptual Model.* Washington, D.C.: Association for Supervision and Curriculum Development, 1973.

it provides for ongoing cooperative, critical analyses of the given meanings of our culture; it promotes the creation of new cultural meanings, as appropriate. Cooperative analysis is a multidimensional process through which women (and concerned others) can disclose contradictions in schooling and society, then move toward critical reflection and cooperative action in the immediate context, be it school or the larger society. New cultural meanings are created in the process.

The framework of analysis includes the dimensions of major social structures, prevailing cultural meanings, and the basic human ways in which people relate to one another. The social structures to be examined include political, economic, and social substructures; aesthetic, metaphysical, and technological rationales and modes of expression; and the communication media, in the broadest sense. Specifics of the cooperative analysis will necessarily be worked out by participants in the context of their immediate realities. As illustration only, I am including a summary of the directions in which such an analysis could move.

1. Political, economic, and social substructures. Focus on the immediate school situation, the community, or the broader social context; ask: who dominates; who is dominant; what purposes are achieved by the given structural relationships; how can the dominated break out of the cycle; do they want to? who can help? what will happen: for example, will the dominated become the dominators? Are women and other oppressed groups participating at serious levels of decision making?

2. Aesthetic, metaphysical, and technological rationales and modes of expression. Whose interests are served by the prevailing modes: are there discernible patterns of inclusion and exclusion? Examine prevailing myths and stereotypes; collectively reconstruct history to correct omissions and falsifications.

3. Communication media. Include texts and other instructional materials as well as newspapers, television, magazines, movies. Consider content, methods of presentation. Whose interests are served? Who makes the decisions? Is there overt or covert sexism or systematic discrimination against any groups through stereotyping, omission, falsification?

4. Participatory skills. Schools can be a liberating force by providing dominated groups with two kinds of skills: the basic "making it" skills for full participation in our technological society:

reading, writing, computation, typing, etc., and the basic political skills and know-how for full participation at serious levels of decision making in our political society. Schools can be an oppressive force by deliberately or implicitly excluding women, and other oppressed groups, from the full acquisition/expression of any or all of the necessary participatory skills.

In the ongoing process of critical analysis of the controlling and manipulative processes of schooling and society, women will be repoliticized. Through collective reflection and cooperative action in transforming the objective conditions of their lives women can transcend given social meanings; produce new knowledge; and initiate open communication about desirable goals of life activity and conduct. I see this process as a way of life, a liberating educational force, an appropriate beginning in women's search for meaning.

3. Schools and Sex
(A Tragedy in Two Parts)

Wm. Burton

THE FUNDAMENTAL CONTRADICTION OF SCHOOLING?

... cold hard plastic edges making sterile indentations
in young flesh alive with joy and ...

The Rules of the School *

Boys must have their hair cut so that it does not overlap their
collars or their eyebrows.

Girls may not wear skirts which come more than 3″ above the knee,
nor may they wear blouses, shirts, or sweaters which do not
meet or overlap the top of their skirts.

Students should wear garments appropriate for their sex.

Students are not allowed to wear shorts, "tank-tops," or other
clothing which leaves uncustomarily large areas uncovered.

Boys must wear sox.

* Quoted from various high school handbooks.

Boys and girls must not hold hands, walk arm in arm, or
   otherwise make displays of affection in public. The school
   is a place for learning, not a place for love affairs.

Students may sign up for the appropriate section of Social Science
   12G or 12B (Marriage, Family, and Sex Education).

Students, particularly girls, who want to get married should
   withdraw from school.

When it is an admitted or confirmed fact that a student is the father
   of an illegitimate child, either born or unborn, or when he
   becomes married to a pregnant girl, he shall be required to
   withdraw from school immediately.

(overheard in passing)

Don't slouch in your seat.

Why can't you walk properly?

My, aren't we casual today?

Did you see how those two were mooning over
   each other?

FLASH ! ! ! ! ! !

The principal today announced his reasons for not allowing
sexually desegregated student smoking areas. He said, "When
I have observed students smoking together in other schools,
there seems to be a lot of mutual wall-leaning which leads
directly to mutual leg-rubbing."
(from a high school underground newspaper)

"Don't . . .

Don't . . .

Don't . . .

Don't . . ."

do a million things which reveal that you are fresh, alive, earthy,
vibrant, indolent, secure, ingenue, and sexy.
Whatever you do—

DON'T BE SEXY

"Even innocent babes cannot endure us, and
we are scarecrows to little children whom
we long to love."

Baudelaire

There they stand. Just as we would be. Just starting—
pregnant—supremely potent beyond our faded capabilities.

A shattering ambivalent challenge.

They are a threat to the existing order of things. The calm
orderly and controlled progression of events is constantly in danger
of utter destruction by their volcanic potential with its unreasonable
risings and irruptions.

Forgetfulness—our fragile protection against onrushing
impotence and death—is shattered by their assumed immortality
worn with a sensual grace.

But, oh the memories they evoke. Memories of power to ...

run

laugh

love

create

. . . . .

once lived

but slipping

faster
faster
faster

away!

Indeed, it is a shattering ambivalent challenge, this youthful
sexuality.

We hate it.
We love it.

It is frightening.
It is beautiful.

It must be controlled.
It must be recaptured.

But how to do both?

DAYDREAMS & NIGHTMARES

The reluctant guru for a generation of teachers speaks:

"The teacher-student relation is almost always erotic; if there is
fear and to-do that it might turn into overt sex, it either lapses
or becomes sick and cruel. And it is a loss that we do not have the
pedagogic sexual friendships that have starred in other cultures.
Needless to say, a functional sexuality is incompatible with our
mass school systems. This is one among many reasons they should
be dismantled."

Paul Goodman

Goodman said that?

Yeah.

You sure?

Yeah.

Where?

The Gay Liberation Book.

Well that explains it.

What?

You know. He's just speaking
as a queer there, not as a
sociologist.

Oh?

Yeah. Teachers just can't go
around making it with students.
They shouldn't and they don't.

Oh?

Favorites

Teacher's pet

> You like her better than you do me, that's why she got an "A."

She is an extremely talented girl who understands better than most the importance of history to a liberal education. She really challenges me and I thoroughly enjoy the time I spend with her.

> Why does that boy upset me so?

> And you must remember, never become too familiar with students.

> One class with that Kid makes getting up in the morning all worth it.

There are many reasons given, many defenses framed, many covers posed; but behind the reasons, defenses, and poses, those "special" relationships go on and on.

"The Coach"
(two versions)

Alright, Kid (pat-pat). I want you to get out there and bust your [vulgar reference to male gonads omitted]. I've put everything into you I can. Now it's time for you to do the job for me (tousle hair). We're in this thing together and I expect everything you've got (hug). Now get your [vulgar reference to human posterior omitted] out there and . . . (pat-pat-smack).

Yes, I'm gonna watch you sweat your [vulgar reference to male gonads] off today (laughter). You're gonna pay me back for that disgrace last night (grimace). You're gonna bust [vulgar reference to human posterior omitted] today—you're gonna hit harder than you've ever hit today—you're gonna run till your [vulgar reference to male gonads omitted] drag the ground today. Today you're gonna prove you're MEN. You're either gonna act like MEN, hit like MEN, fight like MEN, and suffer like MEN, or I'm gonna make you cry for mercy. We're gonna see who's got hair on

their [vulgar reference to human posterior omitted] today.
If you don't, turn in your jock 'cause you don't need it. Now I
want you up for nose-to-nose tackling drills, and I want to see you
love it. I want to hear you love it. I want to hear those bodies smack.
BE MEAN! GET OUT THERE AND HIT!!!

> Poor coach. He doesn't really do anything
> the rest of us aren't guilty of too, does he?
> He's just under more pressure—has less
> time to disguise his actions—is a little bit
> more obvious than most, isn't he?

Why do teachers do what they do—work as they work—
suffer as they suffer?

> the money?
> the prestige?
> the power?

Well, I don't exactly know. I guess I just like kids.

> all kids?   some kids?
> A Kid?

> like?   love?   lust?

Is the answer really so very clear?

> NO?

> NO!

> NO!   NO!   NO!

> NO!   NO!   NO!   NO!   NO!

> WE DON'T

>   (do we?)

The everyday art and literature of our commercial world is a
celebration of our drive to "have" youth. Models for all types of
advertisement currently come primarily from the age group just
below the marketing target, and the trend is to increase this
age disparity.

> (Madison Avenue knows what we won't admit)

We don't—
we don't lust after them

? ? ?

Well, it's not really quite as simple as that.

REPRESSION

may be our salvation
from lusting.

Schools are the unique institutions in which society
systematically attempts to recreate itself. At their very best, they
are profoundly and appropriately conservative.

(Want to scare hell out of a conservative?
What works best? Atheism? Socialism?
Communism? Anarchy? Revolution?
or Sex?)

You said it! It's SEX in a walk!

When the racist wants to conserve the social manifestations
of his values, what worries him most? When the black man . . .

gets a better education?
gets a better job?
goes to white schools?
lives in white neighborhoods?

—or sleeps with a white woman?

The magnitude of the answer is held secret by the earth—
it covers the bodies of black brothers killed for failing to heed
the rage underlying

"How'd y'all lak one o them sleepin with yo daughter?"

You know how it goes. First thing you know, they'll be
wanting to marry whites.

Then there's marijuana.

God knows what it will do to you. But one thing's for sure.
It leads to all that free love stuff. Just look at them hippies.
No morals at all.

Contraceptives?

Abortion?

Sex Education?

Damn it all! What's this world coming to when people
keep trying to make fun out of sex?

(What *did* I say?)

Well, how 'bout it school people. What really scares
hell out of you?

Low test scores?

Unhappy young people?
Noise in the halls?
Kids on drugs?
Too heavy a class load?
Not enough new materials?
Why Johnny can't read?

. . . or little 6th grade Billy quietly enjoying his own body
under the art table without disturbing anyone else?

We're beyond that!

We're beyond that, you say?

Yeah, if we're so liberated about sex, why are we still working
in schools that repress and pervert sex.

Who says?

If we let sex rear its ugly head in the schools at all, we make
damned sure it's a de-eroticized, dehumanized, and thoroughly
mechanized sex.

Why should an M.D. automatically
be the sex-ed instructor?
(S)He may be a lousy lover—
and we never ask.

Check those school rules
again. How many are designed to
directly or indirectly repress sex?

Each society has a coming of age ceremony. Its use is twofold.
It tells the novitiate "The used-to rules no longer hold. Here
are the new rules." The ceremony also extracts a price
from the young for the privilege of joining adult society—
frequently an act of sexual submission by the young to the old.

In our society the rules are always vague
and the circumcision lasts from puberty for
years—and is extracted from both male
and female. Why such cruelty? The
"primitives" have a compassionately short
ceremony?

BUT WE *ARE* LIBERAL!

Masturbation (or, The Salvation of the Young)

Modern educators have come to accept the normalcy of
masturbation, and to understand that this act is a part of
sex life—often into adulthood.

Thus do we demonstrate our concern and affection for
the young

... that we affirm a lonely excursion into
sexual fantasyland as "normal" while
repressing heterosexual intercourse
with undiminished vigor.

... can it be that we have rediscovered
repression-by-tolerance?

Homo-Sex (the crime that just barely dares speak its name during early adolescence)

The acid test for the modern educator dealing with the question of sex is the issue of homo-sex. We affirm that homo-sex can also be considered normal for early adolescents . . .

> so long as it is practiced clumsily, in secret, and without involving affection.

Homo-sex should never endure into adulthood!

There you have it. We love training warriors in the schools— Oh, no? What about high school ROTC? And have you looked at a history text lately?—but we certainly don't want any part of training lovers.

> Why not?

To Teach. . . . . . .
        Teacher. . . . . . .

I learn as much from my students as they do from me.

> Why "from"? Why not "with"?

Well, if you start learning *with* you can get in a lot of trouble. It may wind up being fun. And you know how fun leads to fun.

Learning . . . .
        Loving . . . .

Who ever loved without learning? Why then learning without loving?

> O.K. But only *agape*. *NO EROS!*

> note: the Greeks knew better—and it's their language.

(OFFICIAL TIME OUT)

We really should make a few comments on what is undoubtedly happening by now, that is, the total rejection of this stuff by many of the readers. Why, who's going to seriously entertain the idea that there is anything sexual in the motivation to teach or in a teacher's relationships with young people (except, of course, the emotionally ill). Two comments are perhaps appropriate.

1. Come on! Who are we kidding? We're all alone reading a book that can't tell on us. Why not get up front for once. It is probably good therapy.

2. Try not to fall into the commoditized notion of sex which allows consideration only of acts involving primary plumbing. Sex=sexuality=physicality. There must be times when you want to touch—be physically present with—at least a few.

If not,	If so,
drop out of working with young people (or any people). You're a zombie.	think about which ones and why. Don't disguise it with a lot of pedaguese. Now isn't there a turn-on in there somewhere? Good!

It's funny how we come to believe our own rhetoric, even when it opposes reason and revealed reality.

KIDS & SEX

You'd think (from the rhetoric) that the combination was preordained to be disastrous.

> *Go directly to depravity. Do not pass GO. Do not collect a happy future.*

> But how about our historical reality. A little masturbation, a little homo-sex, and if we were lucky . . .

And here we are,
           still prophesying gloom and doom?

Now really, we simply must get ourselves together.
Talk about reactionary. We want kids to do less sex than we did.
But we're liberal.
We really don't mind.
We tolerate.
                      Besides, why don't you make up your mind.
                      How can you accuse us of seducing children.
                      It looks like we go too far in the other
                      direction.

                 "Methinks the lady doth protest too much."
                            Shakespeare?
        Oh, Stop that now!

As painful as it is to me, I must regretfully inform you that
there is yet a further complication in this whole matter.

            Without a doubt we're having kids. But it's
            coitus interruptus—by vicarious proxy. And
            it's really us (the older folk) that are
            being had—and without being kissed.

It is all quite clear and understandable if three questions are
considered.

1. What is the natural process in sexual gratification?
2. Does society encourage or hinder gratification?
3. If society hinders gratification, whose interests are served
    by the hindrance?

TEACHER'S ANSWER CODE FOR SEX TEST

1. Intercourse (sexual). Also credit copulation, "having sex,"
    "making love." Deduct points for "screwing." Do not credit the
    more commonly used but excessively vulgar expression for
    sexual intercourse. It would be bad moral education.

2. Skip part one as rhetorical. The answer is obviously "hinder."

3. This one will take a little more time—like at least the rest of
    this chapter (life?).

If the school is the institution which
uniquely mirrors society, the family
might be called a cameo of society.
These two hold, hand in hand, the future
of society.

THE FAMILY

HOLY OF HOLIES

all our other gods,

   individual
   democracy
enlightenment

      fall at the feet of ...
         are born only to serve ...

   The family

is it a family of ...

all people?

   all loving people?

     all consenting people?

     NO!

The family is:

(A) a channel for the passing along of accumulated
material goods—thus allowing the wealthy
family to reproduce itself and forcing the poor
family to do likewise.

(B) an economic production unit, especially with the
petite-bourgeoisie and farmers.

(C) the institutional locus for human reproduction

         roughly paraphrased from
         Friedrich Engels (don't dismiss
         it, think about it)

"You can forget about (B). This is the
last half of the 20th century and
everything is big business, including
farming."

"Well (A) is also a little out of date.
That's all that 'ruling class' stuff
and it doesn't take into account the
'managerial revolution' which passed
power from owners to managers."

"It's not quite that simple.
You see . . ."

"Oh, who cares about all that ideological
political stuff anyway. You were talking
about schools and sex. That's a long way
from a political theory of the family."

"Is it really? What about (C)?"

"Sure. Generally, normally, and mostly
children get conceived, born, and reared
in families. So what?"

Well, some people believe that the
family is exactly where people first
learn not to question the class structure
of society.

"Who?"

Wilhelm Reich for one.

"What's his evidence?"

Malinowski's anthropological studies,
mainly.

"What, exactly, does
he claim?"

That the family structure teaches the
young to accept authority automatically,
for one thing.

But more important . . .

The family is the original institution
within which the young learn to trade off
repression of instinctual drives for
material and personal "security"—a very
important lesson if you want to make it
on an automobile production line.

What's an instinctual drive?

> Breathing
> Eating
> and SEX.

> "Be a good girl, Sally, and don't
> *ever* touch yourself there."

GOOD gets SECURITY.
BAD gets REJECTION.   be good

> be good

"Don't be so long in
the bathroom."

> be good "Is that any way for
> a young lady to dress?"

"No! You can't . . .   be good

> read that book.
> see that movie.
be good   go out with him."

> be good   "Save something for marriage."

> "But there *are* liberated parents who under-
> stand that masturbation is normal and
> that . . ."

Same song,
Different verse,
Could'a got better,
but it just got . . . . . .

> the same.

> Want to see a liberal family get conservative?
> Want to see a democratic family go authoritarian?
>
> Try playing "Sex and the Single Kid."

"Well, I know you probably don't understand my position. But
there are some things you'll just have to accept because I
have more experience than you. I understand the consequences
better than you possibly could."

Experience? Ha. That should
be called experience? I should
want to have those experiences?
And those experiences should
make me understand?

In summary, the family performs a two stage political function.
First, it perpetuates a perverted and unnatural sexual morality
which, in turn, creates people unable to live outside this morality.
In short, the family ensures its own reproduction. Secondly, the
family, using this perverted sexual morality as a cornerstone, creates
people who are ever ready to subjugate their own desires to authority
and to equate security with self-denial.

> (For more and better,
> see Wilhelm Reich's
> *The Invasion of Compulsory
> Sex Morality,* and *The Sexual
> Revolution*)

The seed of authoritarianism lies fertile within even the most
liberal of families.

"What a horrible thing to say
about parents who love their
children."

"What?"

"That they pervert them."

"What's wrong with that?"

> We are all perverts. Infirmity and
> perversion are our social normality.
> Gratification is evil. Parents do
> good for their children. Therefore
> parents repress gratification.

> In a universe
> of cripples, a
> whole person is
> a freak.

"Who wants a kid who is
a freak?"

> "Hey, son. How come you always
> have to mess up?"

INSTITUTIONAL SADISM
—family and school

> "This is really going to hurt me
> much more than it will you.
> Someday you will understand that
> I have to whip you because I
> love you."

And someday he will. He will learn
well, and then he'll look around and
say:

What in hell is this society coming to?

Welfare for illegitimate kids and
unmarried mothers.

Contraceptives and abortion on demand.

Sex education *films* in the schools.

Hippie communes with group free love.

Women's liberation.

Legalize homo-sex! I don't care if it is between consenting adults.
Are you crazy? It's all part of an attack on the family and the society.

"Why are 'straight'
people so afraid of
'gay' people?"

"Who says they're afraid?"

"They do—in one way
or another."

FAG

QUEER

WE OUGHT TO BEAT THE ...

"I don't mind as long as they stay with
their own kind. But you can't go too
far. I mean, they have no business
around young people."

"Why not?"

"Kids are impressionable."

"You mean they may get turned on to
homo-sex and off of hetero-sex?"

"Sure."

"Even if they are not so inclined?"

"Sure."

"Why?"

"Damn it. Kids are impressionable."

"You wouldn't want your son taught by
a gay teacher—even if he was an
excellent teacher, then?"

"No. I don't think so."

"Why?"

"I told you. Kids are impressionable.
He might be taken in by that lifestyle."

"If kids are so impressionable, why are
you so worried about one 'gay' teacher
in a whole 'straight' world. Won't he
be much more impressed by the
balance?"

"Well . . ."

Signals
perhaps
from
a deeply buried layer
which still contains
a faded memory
of
what
sexual freedom
might be like

a
chasm
to be
recoiled from.

The greatest fear is fear of the unknown . . .

darkness

death

sex?

Surely no one in her right mind
could claim that sex is an unknown
in this permissive society.

Right. Everyday we get

more talk
more literature
more movies

and more action.

And if you can't get any action,
you can get a manual on how to
improve your technique so you
can
       get
           some
             action.

                 Action?
What kind of
action is
technical
action?

Exactly the
kind we are
getting more
and more of
every day

HI THERE LISTENERS. HAVE YOU MASTERED THE
1001 WAYS OF HAVING SEXUAL INTERCOURSE?
IF NOT, YOU'RE NOT UP TO PLAYBOY AFFICIONADO
STANDARDS. YOU SHOULD . . .

perform
       perform
            perform

  just like general motors

           damn
               they've even made a job
                     out of
                       sex.

    MASTERS AND JOHNSON

            look at it
            when the society wants sex-ed
            it gets an M.D. too.

"Who knows anything about
Masters' or Johnson's
sex life?"

                              and
                               so
                               it
                             goes

                        sublimation

                        masturbation

                        mechanization

(even a little
clumsy and
temporary
homo-sex
early in
life)   anything

                             but

                             the

                             real

                          THING.

    There is no doubt that the nuclear patriarchal family is
declining as an institution in our society. Young people are growing
up much more under the influence of their peers and major social
institutions such as the school and TV than was true with former
generations. More and more the inculcation of values—moral
education—formerly the primary responsibility of the family—
is being formally transferred to the school. The looming question
is what this transfer will do with respect to the values inculcated.

                    "You get a whipping at school and you'll
                    get another one when you get home."

"Don't you think we should consider putting the
children in the Hillanddale School, dear? Their
values are so much closer to ours."

                When you're a kid

                What you sees is what you gets

                            and gets
                            and gets
                            and gets.

What you sees is mainly power.

What you feels is mainly weak.

What you does is mainly conform . . .

                                        to power.

Why in the world would all those
bright, attractive young men
do all those terrible things?

Just doing my duty, Ma'am.

Sieg Heil!

O.K., Mr. Nixon.

> "In our system, state-operated schools may not be enclaves of
> totalitarianism. School officials do not possess absolute authority
> over their students."
>
>   U.S. Supreme Court

Student Rights. Rights, Rights,
Rights. Everybody wants to talk
about their rights. What about
their responsibilities?

> "As for the issue of 'student rights,' all students at Northeast are
> treated commensurate with their general carriage and demeanor,
> and all due respect and deference is given those worthy of it.
> Unfortunately, today, there are many young people who believe
> obedience has nothing to do with freedom. Fortunately the
> administration and majority of the faculty at Northeast realize
> that freedom is the luxury of self-discipline and adherence to a
> proven academic climate."
>
>   33 teachers in a
>   Letter to the Editor

Besides, everyone knows what kind
of people stir up children to
talk about student rights.

> "If only this misguided group of young people knew of the
> insidious influences under which they have fallen, and could
> realize how they are pawns in a master plan of horrendous
> magnitude, then we feel they would be more than glad to
> buckle down to the business at hand . . ."
>
>   33 teachers in a
>   Letter to the Editor

Another mother heard from.

"We would remind these men, the 'Center for Student Rights,'
and the political or perhaps ideological organization financing
this disruptive venture, that they are enticing children without the
permission of their parents. They are, in fact, usurping the
natural rights of parents. . . . One wonders if [****] County
is a pilot project for a new shift in emphasis from the exploiting
of college students to the exploiting of the very young in the
fomenting of new waves of anarchy across our country."

a concerned citizen in a
Letter to the Editor

SEDUCERS! (are they commies or queers?)

> It doesn't matter dummy. Besides,
> they're probably both.

how easily the conventional wisdom correlates
politics and a sexual undertone

is it projection?

(Takes one to know one!)

power and sex
sex and power

repression and seduction
seduction and repression

repression = to have by controlling
seduction = to control by having

Got to learn

to

love
honor
and
obey

That's sure enough the bottom line.

Obey.

But why?

why?

why?

Surely it is not to be contended that all school
people and parents are sadists who are neurotically
compelled to oppress young people.

No, just doing what comes naturally.

What's that?

Holding what you got while you try to get a little more.

What?

You know, keeping the system running since it paid off at least
a little bit.

What system?

The system of AUTHORITY.

Obey:

      the law
        rule
        word

               says the lawmaker.

And like children
we do.

What's wrong with a little respect?

Funny word that.

What?

Respect.

Why?

It always seems to apply only up.

RESPECT

dad

teacher

principal

dean

boss

judge

governor

president

THE FAMILY

THE SCHOOL

THE SOCIETY

arm in arm
into the western sunset
united
at least
in being sure
that

kids

don't

get

normal

sex.

cause kids got to learn to respect. . . .

CUT

Scene: Principal's Office

Actors: Billy, Billy's Teacher, Billy's Dad, Billy's Principal, Billy's
           School Shrink

Teacher: . . . and as I came around to collect the drawings,
            I found him doing that.

Principal: Billy, I'm sure you realize that this is serious
            business. . . .

S. Shrink: Not that there's anything wrong with what you
            were doing. It's perfectly normal. It's just that
            the time and . . .

Father: Well it's not exactly normal—that is—well—lots of
            boys do it—but—well—it's just not the kind of
            thing. . . .

Principal: I'm sure you understand that sex is a wonderful
            and mysterious part of loving, the way two people
            in love create a new human life. . . .

Father: . . . and that's just what everyone is saying. You
            didn't do anything wrong. It's just that—well—all
            that is for later when you're grown up and have
            a wife. . . .

S. Shrink: So you see, Billy, what you were doing is just a
            temporary relief until you are ready for more
            mature. . . .

Teacher: But you just *can not* do *that* in the classroom.

Chorus: BUT THERE'S NOTHING WRONG WITH SEX.

Billy, Billy, Lovely Billy.
You were such a promising lad.
Bright
White
Pretty
Charming
Obedient

What the hell happened?

It just felt so good . . .
    dad
        teacher
            principal
                dean
                    boss
                        judge
                            governor
                                president.

Well damn it son
You've got to learn
to keep your pants on
and work for change
within the system.

And so he did . . .

but he had a hole in his pocket.

Postscript

i'd really like for them to quit
messing over Jes' life.

quit trying to make it a left-over
washed out and faded version of
the mediocrity they were pressed
into.

that would be better for everyone.

but they won't/can't.

so i'll also like it when they don't.

he will know

care

act

to create himself

in solidarity with his sisters and brothers

and that will be good.

4. The Quality of Everyday Life in School

James B. Macdonald

Observation: The teacher was sitting with a group of eight children in a circle on small chairs. Each child was holding a reading book. The children took turns reading aloud to the teacher. She corrected and encouraged them. More often than not the children had to be told where they were supposed to be reading when it was their turn.

In another part of the room nine children were copying a handwriting lesson off the board. There was considerable commotion in this area; especially a great deal of movement and low-toned talk. Three children seemed absorbed in work.

The third group of ten had been given work sheets with structural analysis tasks. They were asked to make new words out of double vowels such as "oo"; and work on endings such as "er," "ing," and "s." Most had either finished quickly and were waiting for further direction, or they had not bothered to do it.

Comment: The actual observation above does not seem unusual in terms of the general quality of existence observed at many levels of schooling over the years. Fundamentally, the hour was characterized by routine, boredom, and busywork. I have often asked teachers why they waste their own and children's lives dealing with trivia and meaningless tasks. I have even accused them of being immoral for doing so! My attitude was summed up by a well meaning principal friend of mine who asked, "How can I change the perspective of my teachers?"

I was wrong, and so was he. We should have been asking, "Who *really* makes the decisions, and *in whose interest* are these boring, routine, and busywork decisions made?"

Everyday Life [1] and Meaning

We live in a modern society which is fundamentally characterized by technology and bureaucracy with an economically consumer-oriented ethic. But society is not simply structures acting upon passive individuals, it creates a concomitant consciousness in individuals which then acts back upon society. It is the kind of modern consciousness that is being developed in schools through everyday life experiences that I wish to explore here.

Consciousness in this context does not refer to the curricular learnings the school intends. The consciousness of everyday life is more tacit or pre-theoretical. It is as Berger [2] says, "the web of meanings that allow the individual to navigate his way through the ordinary events and encounters of his life with others." In toto, they make up his social life-world.

The school is not a primary carrier of the modern consciousness, but along with the mass media serves as a major transmitter of consciousness derived from the primary sources. "Through school curricula, motion pictures, and television, advertising of all sorts . . . the population is continuously bombarded with ideas, imagery, and models of conduct that are intrinsically connected with technological production."

Technological Production

There is a press for technological rationality in the function of the schools. This concept results in attempts to order the nature of teaching functions around the idea that there is a large body of educational knowledge which is potentially available to school staffs, but is organized around a hierarchy of experts. The teachers' activity is seen as a participation in a large organization and as part of the sequence (grade, unit, etc.) of production.

Implicit in this scheme are ideas, such as teacher competency, which suggest that teachers are potentially interchangeable; that productive activity may be learned and performed mechanistically; and that any "good" teaching act is reproducible by another teacher.

---

[1] Many helpful ideas for this essay were stimulated through the works of Henri Lefebvre, especially his *Everyday Life in the Modern World*. New York: Harper & Row, Publishers, 1971.

[2] Peter Berger, Bridgette Berger, and Hansfried Kellner. *The Homeless Mind: Modernization and Consciousness*. New York: Random House, Inc., 1973.

And, finally, that all productive teaching is measurable in terms of the criteria of accountability in use.

The acceptance of this orientation demands that teachers view their work in compartments. Each discipline must be seen separately and each step in the teaching "plan" capable of being broken down and analyzed; then reassembled in a sequentially rational pattern or sequence.

Means and ends are separated also. Since the "knowledge and skills" passed on to students may go into the production of a doctor, a lawyer, a mechanic, or a housewife, the teacher is still capable of performing his or her function without knowing the long-range ends in mind.

Thus, teaching becomes implicitly abstract, that is, it is based upon a frame of reference that is not directly related to the ongoing uniqueness of the everyday life in the classroom, or even to the long-range goals of "production." The "Tyler rationale" is one such abstract decision model: (a) specify objectives in behavioral terms; (b) select activities; (c) organize the activities; (d) evaluate outcomes.

Thus, work for teachers and students is seen as segregated from their private lives. This fractional consciousness not only puts a premium on seeing specific students (and their learning) in terms of problems to be solved, but creates the kind of innovation we have lately experienced as "tinkering." The frame of reference is abstract and not related directly to everyday living.

Social relationships tend to become anonymous and a split in individuals' identities develops. Individuals come to experience themselves in a dual manner: as a private and unique person and as a public functionary. Considerable internal psychological management then becomes necessary and the existence of discipline problems may be largely due to the constant press and struggle to maintain an appropriate dual identity (on the part of either or both teacher and student).

Thus, emotional management and control become extremely important with priority placed upon passive, controlled behavior, acceptant and even-keeled. Then students are incapable of managing their own emotions (that is, split their public and private lives), so the teacher must spend considerable time doing so.

Technological consciousness also leads to prizing optimum growth, or maximum efficiency and effectiveness, the greatest amount of learning in the shortest period of time. This in turn enters the consciousness of students and teachers and helps shape their self-concepts in terms of their relative place in this scheme of things.

Bureaucratic Social Relations

Given a technological orientation, there is an imperative directive to follow out the above kinds of procedures and enter into the modern consciousness of technocracy. Bureaucracy on the other hand does not have the same imperative. Bureaucracy is not intrinsic to a particular goal. Thus, it is possible to witness the displacement of the schools' goals for learning by the functioning of the organizational bureaucracy. School bureaucracies may easily become self-serving. The arbitrariness of much bureaucracy means that contrary to the technological orientation, "production" is not necessarily the major goal.

Thus, schools are political organizations as well as technical producers. The "school" may in fact be almost entirely a politically oriented organization. If this were the case the "school" may actually subvert the technical achievements of learning most efficiently and effectively. The cry for "teacher-free" materials and "deschooling" can be seen as the effects of bureaucracy upon schooling.

The fact of the matter is that schools do exist, they are bureaucracies, and they deflect or support, as the case may be, the general technological consciousness. In the process they create further aspects of the modern consciousness which pervades everyday life.

The bureaucracy of the school deals essentially with the social relations (rather than the technical acts) of the organization. The two are, of course, not unrelated, but any person who has worked with preservice teachers (and many in-service people) will be quick to note that the two overriding concerns of these teachers are "How to teach" (methodology or technology) and "How to manage" (control and organize the social relations in the classroom). In a very real sense these two major concerns reflect the deeply embedded modern consciousness which teachers-to-be have picked up from our modern technological and bureaucratic society.

Bureaucracy creates its own form of knowledge and this knowledge relates to, for example, the definition of roles and status, appropriate agencies, procedures of referral, proper procedures per se, and avenues of redress. Thus, students and staff, in and out of classrooms, must "learn" the rules, procedures, norms, policies, statuses, of the school above and beyond the tasks of technical achievement.

Order becomes the overriding element of bureaucracy. But contrary to the analytical order of production, bureaucratic order is essentially "classificatory." Categorization of students by ability, grade level, unit level, etc., are obvious elements of this phenomenon. The results of ability grouping (in technical terms) are clear indications (that is, generally no significant differences) that the categorization serves primarily bureaucratic order needs and not technical achievement goals.

Bureaucracies are set up to serve clients, not produce "goods." As such the workers of the bureaucracy (school staff members) are always "active," whereas the clients (students) are mostly "passive." Thus, in encountering school bureaucracy the student encounters a general sense of impotence that is not present in his or her later work experience.

Thus, in bureaucracies, in contrast to pure technical production situations, the bureaucrat (teacher) and the client (student) have different goals and problems rather than different perspectives on the same goals. This is a fairly critical distinction that has often been overlooked by educational psychology. The teacher's problem is not "how students learn and develop," as useful as this knowledge could be, but how to construct effective and orderly activities within which students learn and develop. The actual learning and developing are the students' "problems." If the student were not also a living agent in the process the bureaucratic structure could be eliminated and only the goal of the producer (teacher) would be relevant.

Because "desired" relationships are paramount, bureaucracy has a distinctly moral quality that is not apparent in technocracy. The moral quality, however, is an anonymous one, not a personal one. Thus, the axiom of equality among persons within their bureaucratic categories is an axiom of bureaucratic ethics. Further, means are not separable from ends in the bureaucracy of schooling. A student who gets the "right" answer with the "wrong" method, for example, is not appreciated for this achievement.

Consumer Consciousness

The third major characteristic of modern consciousness facilitated by schools is the concern and indeed demand for consumption. The knowledge and skills we produce are made available through bureaucratized social relations for the primary purpose of student consumption. What this entails is a massive publicity operation and a concerted legitimization of the "goods" of schooling. The student by and large does not see the personal need in everyday life for much of what the curriculum deals with. Thus, we psychologize the problem as one of motivation, which results in an analogous function of public legitimization of relatively unneeded "goods," similar to the advertising industry.

Consumption then becomes in schools the substitute for production in real life. What is consumed eventually is the student, not in flesh and blood, but in living time. Thus, it is not difficult to see the consumption of six hours a day for twelve years of a student's life in the act of consuming what are essentially imaginary "goods," that is, abstractions of life rather than productive realities.

This constant consumption has its corollary generalization in the consciousness of the modern person. The act of consumption becomes a good in and of itself, a criterion of worth and "living." What is lost is the consciousness of everyday life in its active, creative, and productive vitality.

Critique to What End?

Decisions about schooling, its form, program, curriculum, in structures and activity, are social policy decisions. They are in fact not appreciably different from legislative acts in their intent. In both cases we assume that the decision will improve the quality of life of the society in some appreciable manner and toward some valued end. Thus, legislative action which makes the Equal Rights Amendment into law is no different in kind (although level and degree obviously vary) than a school system policy decision to remove textbooks which display sexist attitudes or to provide equal funds for girls' athletic programs. Both are (legislative and school policy) social policy decision areas. Thus, school critique is critique of social policy decisions and it is imperative that the end or standard of a critique be made explicit.

The end which I propose as the standard of critique is the quality of everyday living in the schools. This is equivalent to saying that what one needs is essentially a cultural revolution and that economic and political arrangements are key variables or means toward those ends.

In schools the analogy to broader economic variables is related to such things as the curriculum, social access to learning, equitable allotments of materials, personnel, and resources. The "economy" of the school is mirrored in the learning tasks (*work*) and all its contributing factors. This often is the realm of the technical.

Political processes in the schools are analogous to party politics, law, and access to power in decision making. In schools it is reflected in the policies, management practices, patterns of interpersonal relationships, and social control mechanisms. The "politics" of the school is most often the realm of the bureaucratic.

Yet changing the "economy" or the "politics" of the school is only a public means toward the end of a change in the cultural conditions and private quality of life. If these are seen as ends in themselves they tend toward polarizing ideologies and change takes on a tendency toward "inversion." Thus, the swings back and forth in curriculum innovation over the past century appear to be due to mistaking the "economic" and "political" as innovative ends rather than analytical and practical means of reaching a higher quality of existence, through reuniting the public and private aspects of living.

This is true, I would argue, in Western society at large, where Socialist doctrine (originally grounded in a *social*-ism) aimed at making the quality of one's social existence as humanly fulfilling as possible but which has been short-circuited by Socialist acceptance of change in public economic policy and political control as the ends, rather than reintegration of the public and private realms through cultural change. Thus, we tend to see the same technological and bureaucratic domination of everyday life in, for example, both Russia and the United States. Somewhere along the line the means have become the ends. The Western democratic processes and capitalistic economics and Western Communist party processes and socialist economics are in neither case sufficient as ends in themselves. They are only as valid and meaningful as they contribute to the quality of cultural experience—of everyday living. Both "worlds" may be faulted heavily for destroying everyday living reality. That they are more similar in this respect than different is readily seen in the policy of "detente"—a reflection of the easy movement of technical and bureaucratic consciousness and meaning structures between the two worlds.

Loss of Personal Living in Schooling

The source of meaning of the schools in society and the source of meaning for persons engaged in schooling resides in the human activity that takes place in the school. We have for too long paid attention to the rhetoric of goals, objectives, and product assessment as if these statements or measurements reflected the fundamental meaning.

That this is not so is now patently clear. Meaning resides within persons regardless of the societal traditions, social conditions, or verbalized goals. Traditions, conditions, and goals are merely boundaries and directives that enter into the shaping of activity, they do not represent the meaning of activity itself. If we are to understand the meaning of the schools we must search for the social meaning of the human activity that takes place there; and if we wish to examine the meaning implications of schooling we must look at the personal activity of people in the schools.

This is not necessarily the same thing as saying that "we learn by doing" or that "all learning is experientially based." The concern here is not for learning in its traditional sense, but for the development and/or explication of meaning structures in human consciousness which are inherent in the activity itself and not necessarily what is learned from that activity.

Let us look first at the activity in the schools in our society and then move toward reflection on the social and personal meanings of that activity.

Activity in schools, according to Philip Jackson,[3] may be characterized by the phenomena of (a) unequal power, (b) living in groups or crowds, and (c) evaluative or judgmental qualities in relation to activity and rewards.

What this in effect means is that all school activity is controlled by the staff; in the sense that even the power to let students exercise control is given to them by teachers or other staff. Further, it means that all activity has a social meaning. Every activity has implicit connective tissue among the people engaged in schooling. And, still further, all activity is constantly being evaluated and judged in process through the normative threads of at least three kinds: (a) the effect of activity on others; (b) the desired direction of activity in terms of those who control; and (c) the "objective" utility of the patterns by which activity is shaped. Thus, the major concerns of teachers are easily understood as discipline (or control), methodology, and content: (a) what to teach; (b) how to teach it; and (c) how to control the social behavior of the students. Thus, schools pattern activity, direct its flow, and monitor the social relationships within the process.

At this level of analysis it makes little if any difference what the substantive nature of the activity might be, for example, arithmetic or music; it is the formative character of the activity that

[3] Philip Jackson. *Life in Classrooms.* New York: Holt, Rinehart and Winston, Inc., 1968.

guides the development, the personal meaning, and the interpretation of its social meaning. Thus, if we are to understand what school "means," socially and personally, we must understand the formative quality of the activity that takes place there, not simply the substantive learning outcomes of this activity.[4]

It is in fact the phenomena of school activity that are the primary justification for having schools at all. If the substantive quantity of learning were the primary concern, we have within our technical power a variety of ways to transmit knowledge and develop skills. In fact, we could most likely with certain creative rationalization such as Ilich's Learning Webs, cable TV, or community learning centers, do a better and more equitable job of the substantive learning than is now attempted in schools.

The activity in and of the school is not neutral. The activity embodies the quality of experience which infuses and symbolizes meaning rather than the quantity of learning; and as school people we have tended to accept our practices in a framework of technical neutrality. Thus, school people have mistakenly thought that in their practices, activities, and aims they are value free (or perhaps better—free of having to commit themselves to values). This misguided "centrist tendency" has actually resulted in an acceptance of broader social values which are destructive of the development of personal meaning and which are representative of a form of oppressive social meaning.

Thus, the activity characterized above is reflective of and communicative of social meanings inherent in the social power structure of the broader society. In this context the criticism of the "mindlessness" of the schools takes on a powerful meaning. It is a mindlessness which does not critically identify the public behaviorist values embodied in the activity of schooling. It is a mindlessness that continues to accept through its practical activity a process by which persons are alienated from one another and from their own potential as human beings. This in turn makes the dominant social meanings ones which foster the oppression or dehumanization of other people; and is seen as a natural way of existing because it has been created in the "natural" context of the activity of school life.

4 "Formative" and "substantive" are used here in an analogous sense to the way Jean Piaget uses them. Thus, the formative aspects refer to basic private developmental growth and not the arbitrary substantive content of a given society. In this sense the formative base of everyday living develops attitudes, feelings, dispositions, and cognitive orientations rather than the specific substantive content of the curriculum.

The schism between our liberal rhetoric and our own practices is easily seen to be related to the mindlessly oppressive character of school activity which accompanies the discussion of our higher values. Thus, we study justice in an activity context characterized by injustice. As, for example, our knowledge of the tradition of justice grows, our ability to act justly decreases through the implicit meaning structures of the learning activities. Thus, we leave schools knowing about justice, and "that" justice is a good thing; but knowing "how" to unjustly oppress people effectively.

On the personal side of the picture the corollary of social oppression (our acting out of practice in relation to others) has other destructive effects. Inwardly the activity of the schools represses the uniqueness of our own meaning structures. Our personal meanings are consistently delegitimated through the activity of schooling, and this is not the same as losing an argument or having an unresolved conflict of values in an open situation.

The exercise of unequal power, the use of praise and blame in group settings, and the general judgmental aura of the school activity clearly communicate that the personal meanings of the person are not legitimate for common sharing with others. Further, the expression of personal meaning under these circumstances involves high risk on the part of the student.

Personal meanings when expressed or felt thus become anxiety laden and often result in guilt or shame reaction when not accepted or praised. As a result individuals engage in a "forgetfulness" concerning their own meanings. Thus, they repress or submerge the unique meaning structure growing out of their own activity and take on the attitude and posture of the control agent.

When this happens the students have completed the personal-social connection by an accommodation to social alienation with the added dimension of becoming alienated not just from others or their work, but also alienated from their own personal potential through repressive "forgetfulness."

Personal response to this process is reasonably predictable and is characterized by student withdrawal and passivity, lack of initiative, and destructive personal coping behaviors such as "apple polishing" or "schoolmanship." These behaviors are personally destructive of individual meaning structure regardless of how well they adapt one to the oppression and alienation of the school activity that is implicitly reflective of the "neutral" stance of the school.

Anger and aggression are further predictable behaviors in such circumstances, although they appear not to be as prevalent as withdrawal and destructive coping simply because the unequal power situation provides much greater risk to the aggressive student.

In the long run it is certainly reasonable to predict that constant immersion in the dominantly characteristic school activity contributes to neurosis, psychosis, fanciful romantic nonsense, drug experience, and social violence. Having systematically submerged one's own meaning structure for years, the hope of self-realization (or making oneself more real) becomes less possible in the usual context of social activity.

The struggle for personal meaning goes on within persons, but if we have done our job well, students are effectively cut off from the personal sources of their own creativity and growth, and accommodated to an alienated view of the social world. Thus, the person who attempts to exercise choice and direction, lacking clear personal grounding or adequate social reality frameworks, creates further socially and personally destructive behavior. Thus, the hope of developing or facilitating the development of responsible personal meaning structures and activity becomes less and less likely.

Contradictions in Schooling

When the technological, bureaucratic, and consumer ethos enter the consciousness of staff and students the personal activity of everyday living, the fundamental quality of existence, becomes counterfeit and is replaced by a kind of "false consciousness." This "false consciousness" can be seen clearly when we look at certain contradictions which are revealed in traditional everyday school living activity. The contradictions are viewed in terms of what Habermas [5] has called the three aspects of practical activity: (a) work, (b) power, and (c) language. The contradictions are, of course, grounded in the acceptance of the quality of living as the cultural end of social policy. In other words, we must assume that the answer to the basic question, "In whose interest is the activity of the school?" presents contradictions when the form and quality of work, power, and language create conflicts between the everyday living interests of those experiencing the activity, and other explicit or implicit external agencies imposing school activity in the service of their own interests.

Contradictions in Work ("Economics")

1. "Seriousness vs. irrelevance and triviality." Work in the schools for teachers and students is supposed to be serious and

[5] Jürgen Habermas. *Theory Into Practice.* Boston: Beacon Press, 1973.

"task oriented"—a *serious* business. Teachers are expected to be professional about their jobs, to know and possess the correct rhetoric. They are thus expected to take their job seriously, to serve the students and the system. Schooling is to be seen by students as the most serious and important event in their social lives.

Students are expected to take school seriously. Discipline problems and other disruptions which interfere with the seriousness of learning are cardinal sins. Further, students who lack "motivation" or school game playing skills are a constant irritant to the business at hand.

The contradiction lies in the fact that there is a general lack of conviction about the standards and worthwhileness of tasks imposed in the schools. Many teachers wonder "why" they are teaching what they are to disinterested youngsters. Promotion is more than likely automatic no matter what youngsters achieve. Graduation is usually a test of endurance for nonacademically oriented students. However, the compulsion to act "seriously" is still felt by all involved.

What this does is debase the nature of labor or work in the schools. It clouds the development of values in the productive activity of the persons there, since all work must be taken seriously whether clearly justified or not. As a result, people become alienated from their work because the pleasure of worthwhile activity is reduced to satisfaction in the external rewards offered in the absence of justifiable standards. Everyday life loses its potential reality as persons in schools become divorced from a sense of worth in their activity.

2. "Consumption of quantities of 'goods' vs. production of quality in work." The industrial ideology of consumption of material goods is reflected in the structure of school activity inasmuch as schools emphasize the quantitative accumulation (or consumption) of skills and knowledge. It is correlated with the idea of expansion rather than development, growth rather than progress or balance.

Schools assume that the more one knows, the better one consumes and accumulates skill and knowledge, the better one becomes. Thus, as in society, a continuous accumulation becomes the end in itself.

Opposed to this is the idea that the quality of productive work enhances human development in schooling, and skills or knowledge are part of the contributing means for this development. This contradiction is as old as the Socratic and Rhetoric schools of thought—

men of virtue or men of consummate skill (that is, knowledge + technique). It is also as new as the present concern for formative aspects of moral and intellectual development rather than the substantive outcomes of morals and intellect.

People in schools experience life as the facilitation and acquisition of a never-ending accumulation of substantive outcomes. Whether or not they contribute to the personal quality of human development is not a major concern. Teachers and other staff even experience their own professional growth as the accumulation of courses and credentials, and not in terms of the increasing quality of their own professional work and personal development.

In effect then the activity of the classroom is coercive in the use of power since the emphasis upon accumulation of the past divorces people from their own sense of development in the present and they must be "motivated," "structured," and "controlled" in order to foster brute accumulation.

Work is divorced from the everyday meaning structures of the individual. Accumulation as a goal demands dependence upon external rewards, not the developmental relevance of present activity, which provides intrinsic reward.

Verbal acquisitions, as concepts, ideas, facts, or skills, are seen as the major "goods" to be accumulated. These acquisitions are not viewed basically as a means to enlightenment and development. As such they deal fundamentally with language about language rather than common language (words about the reality of immediate activity).

Once again, everyday living and the quality of development are devalued by the accumulative consumption ideology of the schools.

3. "Compartmentalization of work vs. lived experience of wholeness and continuity in activity." Compartmentalization of activity takes place in terms of time, behavior, and task in the schools. Thus, we are able in the interest of outside agencies to "divide and conquer" the young by adult compartmentalization of subject matter, by external sequencing and limitation of true involvements, and by dividing behavior (and shaping objectives) in cognitive, affective, and psychomotor realms. The rationale for these compartmentalizations is of course not available through the lived experiences of the young.

This in effect detaches the work of students in school from their own sense of wholeness and experiential continuity. The quality of their engagement and the sense of control over their experience are submerged in the imposition and compartmental manipulations of their work experience.

Inherent in this procedure is the technically rational planning and organization of work tasks and pupil activity which, in the interests of others, destroys the spontaneity, creativity, playfulness, and essential risk-taking potentials of everyday living experiences.

Contradictions in Power ("Politics")

1. "Compulsion for order vs. the ideology of democracy." Democratic processes, and especially the sharing of power through participation, are cornerstones of democracy. In schools as in many other places of work the Bill of Rights is effectively "parked at the door."

Democracy becomes politicized through this process and is removed from the everyday living of the participants. It becomes an abstraction that is not lived, but talked about.

The perceived need for order which has become almost a compulsion preempts democratic processes. Thus, the compulsion to have things run smoothly, to be efficient, to be accountable for goals, and thus to control the social behavior of students contradicts the meaningful embodiment of real, everyday democratic living in classrooms.

As a result the quality of human relationships is infused with a hierarchical domination in everyday life. In the process democracy loses its everyday meaning as power is abstracted from living and exercised authoritatively. In the process work tasks and human relations are imposed for the sake of order.

Closely correlated with this contradiction is the ideology of "maturity" which both legitimates imposed order and seduces the student. Full participatory living and sharing of power are denied on the basis of the "maturity of the adult" (or immaturity of the student). This rationalization allows adults to impose their order on the student and at the same time allows the student certain "immature" trade-offs in behavior. Thus, students are not expected to be "responsible" for many kinds of behavior because they are immature.

In effect, classroom life becomes (again) a form of activity abstracted from everyday life. The consequences of behavior are sheltered from reality because students learn they are immature, and the imposition of activity is legitimated because adults are "mature."

2. "Social reward of satisfaction vs. personal reward of pleasure." The need for order and bureaucratic control, abstracting

personal participation from its lived practice, necessitates a concomitant abstract reward system.

Whereas in the everyday life of experience reward comes through the personal pleasure gained from productive activity, it is now necessary to legitimate imposed activity by "teaching" a substitute and abstracted need for rewards that are socially satisfying rather than personally pleasurable.

Students, thus, work for grades, teacher approval, test results, parental approval, and to competitively best other students. These rewards are not "in the interest" of students in terms of the intrinsic value of activity in their everyday lives. They provide a pale copy of pleasure in the form of satisfaction (or socially abstracted pleasure).

Satisfaction is in the "pleasing" of others and the achievement of rewards which have future "meaning" rather than direct meaning in everyday life. Thus, slowly, students lose their own sense of value in activity and substitute social satisfactions which make them dependent upon abstract rewards for their sense of worth.

By the age of nine or ten this reward system has been completely internalized, most creative behavior has been repressed, and the alienation of the "losers" (predominantly the lower classes) has become almost complete. It is clear that the substitution of social satisfaction for personal pleasure in the interest of persons and processes outside the living context of the school diminishes the quality of lived experience there.

Contradictions in Language ("Culture")

1. "Disembodied intellect vs. organismic presence." In everyday life communication in its cultural context is a complete organismic response involving facial gesture, bodily posture, emotional mood, tacit understanding, and personal organic needs. The activity of the school in contradiction focuses almost entirely upon formal structures of communications, primarily language. Thus, the curriculum goals are essentially divorced from the concrete biology of the student.

It is not simply that the school justifies its role in terms of the intellectual development of the student. This, again seen from the point of view of the quality of everyday life, is a form of compartmentalization of abstraction from practical living. The school, its rewards, and its tasks become focused upon a highly restricted (though highly socially useful) set of human capacities. In a fundamental sense the student as organism is disembodied in the process, since even primary bodily functions such as erotic pleasures, elimination, and ingestion are ordered and subordinated to verbal learning goals.

The body, when recognized at all, is relegated to a segmented physical education consisting in most cases of exercise gained through the enduring of a social games and skills oriented program.

This divorcement of the verbal from affect and psychomotor activity provides a highly useful control and sorting mechanism for society, but in the process destroys the fabric of everyday living in the sense of full organismic participation in life. In the process it helps teach students to distrust their own values, emotions, and bodies as basic aspects of life and to this extent diminishes the full meaning of being alive.

2. "Language as words about words vs. language as words about reality." The verbal focus of the schools is further destructive of full living to the extent that the primary emphasis is not related to connecting language activity to concrete experience, to self-expression in the act of full participation in living; but to manipulating words whose referent is other words. The development of the language experience approach to teaching reading is one such recognition of this fundamental contradiction. In this case learning to read is hopefully connected to concrete experience of the students' immediate lives.

But beyond certain early practices, the school curriculum quickly becomes a "definitional" experience. That is, previous words are utilized as the referent for constructing and understanding new words (or ideas). In a very real way this results in a means of masking or mystification of the understandings hoped for rather than revealing meaning to the student through verbal processes that serve their own practical possibilities.

There can be no quarrel with the need for words about words at some point in schooling. But the fact of the matter is that this approach is fundamental and pervasive throughout schooling. Further, as presently operational it is essentially self-defeating since it rejects the building of language in concrete reality and divorces meaning structures from active potentials of human beings.

Again, it is useful to ask "in whose interest" this process operates—for it is clear that it basically contradicts the goal of developing full, active meaning structures related to the practical everyday life of students; and thus is not an enhancement of their own development and the quality of their living.

In conclusion, further exploration of life in schools could uncover other contradictions, perhaps even more important than those examples provided here.

The fundamental point of this analysis is the highlighting of contradictions between things deemed important in the schools and the quality of living in the schools. And, if we accept the improvement of cultural conditions of everyday life as the fundamental goal of social change (that is, the enhancement of the quality of existence), then the resolution of contradictions becomes a first order of business for schooling. The pattern of these contradictions is of course not unique to the schools. The same kinds of contradictions can be seen in our other technological, bureaucratic, consumer oriented institutions throughout our society.

The analysis of schooling from the viewpoint of the everyday life in the schools leads me to the conclusion that fundamental attempts to "re-form" the schools must focus upon the activity in the schools as a cultural milieu, with the technical and political concerns as major means for constructing environments that enrich the quality of living.

This proposed conclusion is both value oriented and practical. That is, it reflects a basic concern for cultural change rather than technical or political change, per se; and it reflects a practical conviction that what we are best able to change (should we wish to) is the activity of schooling, rather than change in the "outputs" brought about by technical acts.

If we wish to get at the root of the problem of schooling, that is, take a radical approach, it would seem to be clear that a cultural re-forming is the end goal and that this cultural reform must deal directly with human activity in its qualitative aspects.

5. On Contradictions in Schools

John S. Mann

EXTERNAL EVENTS PROVIDE the *conditions* for change: internal contradictions within a thing provide the *basis* of change.[1] This is a fundamental principle of dialectical materialism. Our concern with contradictions in this chapter is not some new academic toy. It reflects a commitment to change that is serious enough to lead out of the quagmire of spontaneous off-the-cuff speculation and into the use of systematic tools.

Dialectical analysis of the contradictions within a thing as the *basis* for change, and the relation of these contradictions to the *conditions* for change, is a method that has an unlimited range of application, and has achieved enormous practical results. The application of this method to social development over time is known as historical materialism which is the philosophical basis of all Marxist thought.[2]

Since the turn of the century, Marxist analysis of our world political and economic situation has focused upon three contradictions as the basis for social progress in our epoch. These are: the contradiction between labor and capital; the contradiction between imperialist, colonizing, or oppressor nations and subject, colonized, or oppressed nations; and the contradictions between rival imperialist nations.

[1] Mao Tse-tung. "On Contradictions." *Selected Works of Mao Tse-tung.* Peking: Foreign Languages Press, 1967.

[2] The clearest brief explication of historical materialism is: Joseph Stalin. *Dialectical and Historical Materialism.* New York: International Publishers Company, Inc., 1940.

These contradictions do not exist apart from each other. They are dialectically related. Thus, for example, the contradiction between labor and capital results in crises within capitalist countries with certain regular features like overproduction of goods and loss of consumer purchasing power. Also when certain vast areas have not yet developed advanced methods of production, the contradiction between labor and capital necessarily results in the development of imperialism.

The three contradictions, then, are interconnected. But, the heart of the matter is the first one, the contradiction between the interest of those who live off the profit of ownership and those who live by selling their labor power, their capacity to produce goods, to the owners.

All this may seem out of place in a yearbook on curriculum, and far removed from the educator's concern for schools and school children. Yet it is not. It is precisely the view that school problems can be "solved" without reference to such things as class structure and imperialism that has kept well-intentioned educators impotent. In his forthcoming book, Jonathan Kozol talks about the "myth of no connections" with which we indoctrinate our children. Educators themselves are victims of the same "myth," or more accurately, the same ideology; the ideology of "reform"; the ideology that says we can correct the evils resulting from class structure without understanding and overturning that class structure. My premises as an educator are: that the fundamental problems in schools are best explained and acted upon in terms of an analysis of contradictions within the schools; that the contradictions within schools are manifestations of the contradictions in society in general; and that the larger society constitutes the conditions for change within the schools.

This means, generally, that progressive movement in schools is part of, and not apart from, progressive movement in society; and in particular, it means that schools are one specific area of class struggle and that progressive educators are by definition engaged in class struggle. A great deal of energy has been expended (for example, under the ideology of professionalism) to blind educators to this fact, with the result that a major characteristic of the professional educator is his or her inability to recognize or interpret the failure of reformist movements to change schools with respect to their basic functions. But for me, the main purpose of this yearbook is to help radical educators out of the trap of reformism. The way to do this is to expose the class basis of the contradictory tendencies in schools—to show that the public schools are objectively a massive system controlled by the owning class which uses the system to disseminate its ideology and to shape and manage the potential labor force it will exploit in future years; to show that opposition to this kind of schooling entails opposition to the owning class and its interests; to show that education is thus an instrument of class struggle, a tool in the combat between the class that rules and the classes and peoples that are exploited—to show, finally, that educators have a clear-cut choice between serving the ruling class by being its functionaries in the school system and serving the interests of the exploited and oppressed.

Ruling class interest is expressed in schools in three forms: control of ideology, control of knowledge, and control of training for the work force. In each of these areas, the interest of the ruling class is in direct contradiction to the interest of people who will be exploited by the ruling class throughout their adult life. This contradiction is the basis for change in schools.

Ruling Class Ideology in the Schools

At the heart of ruling class ideology is a falsification of the meaning, the history, and the concrete condition of democracy in the United States.

First Falsification

That the basis for the struggle for democracy that came to a head in 1776 was a set of "ideals" rather than a set of economic interests. This falsification is in the interest of the ruling class because it leads directly to the belief that the institutions set up by our "founding fathers" were and continue to be democratic in a pure and ideal sense and that our problems reflect the errors or weakness of this or that individual. A corollary of this belief is that problems can be corrected by getting better people into the institutions without changing the institutions. Thus, this falsification protects the ruling class from any assault on the institutions that serve them.

In contradiction to this set of beliefs is the reality that our institutions were created through the struggle of what 200 years ago was the emerging mercantile class to protect and advance its material interests. Thus, the political "philosophy" of John Locke, upon which so much ruling class ideology is based, was a rationalization of the interests of the progressive new class.[3] And the institutions established by that class were not pure democratic institutions but rather were institutions designed to assure the continued freedom of that class. The foundation of all our institutions, the constitution of the United States, establishes property as the basis of law. In its time, the constitution was progressive in that it expanded the property rights, and thus the democratic political rights, of an emerging and expanding new class—the owning, or bourgeois class. But it was regressive with respect to the enormous propertyless class of workers created through the dialectical development of this new owning class.

The idealist view of democracy says that our institutions are based on philosophical ideals. The materialist view says that our institutions arose from the concrete material struggles of a new class rising to power. The first view protects the ruling class. The second view gives the oppressed classes a basis for assaulting institutions rather than "bad" individuals.

Look at the textbooks, look at the Pledge of Allegiance, listen to the casual remarks about democracy made by teachers, and decide which view of democracy is being taught to our children— the idealist or the materialist. It is impossible to separate these views from the concrete interests of two classes—the very small minority ruling class and the massive working class.

Second Falsification

That the U.S. Constitution establishes "pure democracy," that is, democracy for all regardless of race, class, creed, sex, etc. Whereas the first falsification protects the ruling class from attacks upon institutions, the second protects the ruling class from attacks directly upon itself. As long as the ideology prevails that our system of government is in principle designed to serve and protect all people equally, people with grievances will believe that the system itself will ultimately support them and that remedy, therefore, lies entirely within the system. The facts, and the interests of all oppressed and exploited people, however, contradict this belief. Our constitution, as Charles Beard amply demonstrated in his exhaustive study,[4] was written by white propertied men and had as its primary function

[3] The relations between Locke and the Mercantilists, particularly the prominent Lord Shaftesbury, is sketched out in: W. A. Williams. *Contours of American History.* London: Jonathan Cape, Publishers, 1961.

[4] Charles Beard. *An Economic Interpretation of the Constitution of the United States.* New York: The Free Press, 1935.

the protection of the rights of property from both the royalty of the past and the dispossessed working classes and national minority peoples of the future. The constitution and all the government apparatus built upon it are democratic with respect to one class and undemocratic with respect to other classes. Above all else, it protects the rights of owners, of the owning class. Possession, the adage says, is 9/10 of the law.

Our democracy, like Athenian democracy and other historical instances of democracy, is not pure or absolute democracy but only relative democracy. Relative not in the sense of being imperfect due to human fallibility, but systematically relative in the sense that it is democratic for the owning class and undemocratic for the non-owning classes, for the working classes, the classes that earn their living through productive labor rather than through interest and profit derived from appropriation of the value created by others. That is how the owning class gets to be the ruling class. If the masses in this country were taught that we have relative democracy, democracy that systematically protects and enfranchises the owning class absolutely, but protects and enfranchises other classes only relatively, then the relation between one person's poverty and another person's wealth would be more readily understood, and then the oppressed would be ideologically free to seek remedy by attacking the ruling class. Where in schools is the class basis of U.S. democracy taught? In which social studies curricula is the full meaning of "possession is 9/10 of the law" examined? And conversely, what educator has not seen endless examples, in both the formal and tacit curriculum, of the teaching of the ruling class ideology, the teaching of the false proposition that our democracy in principle is pure democracy, is equally democratic for all?

These two instances by no means exhaust the list of falsifications about U.S. democracy that occur in the schools; but they are the bulwark of ruling class ideology. It is on the basis of these two falsifications that so much other ideology rests—the ideology of equal opportunity, or the ideology of "liberty and justice for all."

Closely associated with control of ideology is control of knowledge. In fact, in the two preceding sections, I have indicated that sustaining the dominance of ruling class ideology entails falsification of history. This is not a "conspiratorial" theory of class struggle. It is not a matter of a clique getting together in a room somewhere deciding how to falsify history in order to sustain ruling class ideology. The relation between knowledge and ideology is more complex, more dialectical than that. Ideology both determines and is reinforced by the way facts are regarded, selected, interpreted. While the process of control of knowledge must not be analyzed simplistically, the objective fact remains that knowledge is controlled in the interest of the ruling class; that there exists within the school system a contradiction between its control of knowledge in the interest of the ruling class and the dispensation of knowledge that would be in the interest of exploited and oppressed people. The most important areas in which knowledge is controlled are:

1. History of class struggle
2. National minority history, language, and culture
3. Historical materialism
4. Health, technology, and science.

This list is not exhaustive, but a brief discussion of each of these areas may help educators see the relation between knowledge and class struggle.

History of Class Struggle

In the study of history, the chief question to keep in mind is "for whom?" In any historical epoch, the ruling class rationalizes its actions in metaphysical language that disguises its self-interest. Kings rule by "divine right" in the name of "God." Early U.S. industrial interests (railroads, mining, processing of raw materials) steal the land from Native Americans through genocidal policies rationalized as "manifest destiny." Modern U.S. capitalists plunder riches around the globe in the name of protecting "democracy" in the free world. In school, the dominant approach to history entails acceptance of this type of explanation of historical events, and never asks "for whom?"—never directs attention to the fact that the class of people who formulate policy and the class of people who propagate the rationale and the class of people who profit directly from the policy are one and the same class.

Thus, children are deprived of the fundamental principle of historical development and historical inquiry; the principle that history is guided by the dialectical struggle of conflicting class interests, and that idealist "explanations" rationalize, but do not explain, events.

In U.S. history, while the more liberal approaches express some moral concern for the victims of chattel slavery, wage slavery, and land appropriations, these are shown as unfortunate by-products rather than as intrinsic components of the system of "free enterprise." The system itself is "democracy" and "freedom," so how could it entail slavery, robbery, and genocide? Yet the facts of history, which are withheld from us, make it clear that slavery, robbery, and genocide were the absolute basis for the rise to supremacy of U.S. industry. And consequently, the facts also make it clear that the system called—rationalized as—"democracy" and "free enterprise" is a system devised in the interest of a new ruling class and against the interest of the robbed, exploited, and liquidated peoples. If history were taught as the working out of the problem of "for whom?" there would be serious consequences. Masses of people would see that our system, in spite of being called "democracy" and "free enterprise," is intrinsically not in their interest but is in the interest of the profiteers of the system. Exploited people would become conscious of their interests as a class, and of the contradictions between their interests and the interests of the ruling class. Then they might ask "what system and what form of struggle are in our interests?"

A corollary to the disguising, in historical study, of the interests of the ruling class is a disguising of the class-conscious struggles of the exploited. Resistance to or rebellion against capitalism, when it is taught at all, is most often taught as isolated events. The liberal treatments emphasize the outrageous condition that this or that particular group of people had imposed upon them at some particular time. The more orthodox treatments yield that there was some ground for complaint, but that outright rebellion is uncalled for, and is led by nuts, fanatics, and troublemakers. Neither treatment gives students knowledge of the continuity of struggle against capitalist exploitation, knowledge of the place of particular rebellions in the overall historical development of class struggle, knowledge of the class interest of *all* exploited people in a particular rebellion of a few people, knowledge of the class-conscious leadership of rebellion, knowledge of the general economic conditions surrounding a rebellion, knowledge of the vital interests of the profiteers that were threatened by rebellion and of the absolute ruthlessness with which rebellion is suppressed, knowledge of the systematic and unrelenting tactics employed to prevent, break up, subvert, and destroy rebellion before it gets to the point of attracting publicity. Knowledge, in short, of the continuing class struggle between owner and exploited, between labor and capital, is suppressed.

Show me a text that honestly portrays class struggle in the United States and I will show you a text that will not be used, except in occasional moments of confusion, in the "public" schools. Show me a teacher who honestly teaches the history of class struggle, and I will show you a teacher who will not be long employed in the "public" schools. Knowledge of history is controlled by the owning class, the bourgeoisie, and in contradiction to their interest in knowledge of history is the interest of the masses of exploited people in the knowledge of their history as a class, as Marx says, not only *in* itself but *for* itself.

National Minority History, Language, and Culture

In the course of its development, this country has both captured and incorporated and created within its boundary a number of nations and peoples. The various Indian peoples, the peoples of the Southwest, the Puerto Ricans, and the Filipinos are examples of incorporation and conquest. The Negro nation is an example of a nation created during the process of U.S. development.[5] Just as it is in the interest of the ruling class to conceal the lines of class struggle in order to undermine the attack on itself as a class, so too is it in the interest of the ruling class to conceal and confound the lines of national struggle in order to undermine the attack on itself as the source of imperialist national conquest. The characteristics of a nation are territory, culture, economic base, language, and psychological makeup as a reflection of culture and economic base. Consciousness of nationhood, which entails consciousness of the right of independence from exploiting imperialist nations, entails consciousness of these five common characteristics that bind the people of a nation together.

Conversely in defending its position as an imperialist power, it is in the interest of the ruling class of the United States to undermine those aspects of nationhood that would call attention to the right of subject nations to independence. Thus imperialism attacks those aspects of nationhood both objectively and subjectively:[6] objectively, by destroying the culture, the economic base, the

[5] The basis for recognition of the Negro Nation in the South of the United States is presented in: *The Negro National Colonial Question.* Detailed study published by the Communist League.

[6] Imperialism also *creates* nations. The dialectical relation between the creation and the destruction of nations under imperialism is too complex for presentation in this essay. See: V. I. Lenin. *Imperialism: The Highest Stage of Capitalism.* Peking: Foreign Languages Press, 1973.

language, and the psychological makeup; subjectively, by destroying awareness of these. Schools play a critical role in this strategy. Objectively, they contribute directly to the destruction of culture, language, and psychological makeup. In the Southwest, for example, where I have been teaching for three years, schools have traditionally practiced corporal and psychological punishment of children who spoke Spanish in school or who overtly expressed their Mexican national culture. Psychological makeup is caricatured and debased by calling children who do not conform to the Anglo-American model "lazy Mexicans."

And subjectively, in addition to undermining children's respect and love for their own language, culture, and people the schools help to obliterate any lingering sense of territory or economic integrity by teaching history from the point of view of the greatness of "America's" drive West under the doctrine of manifest destiny, and by stressing assimilation into the U.S. economy.

In recent years, under the impact of ruling class politicians in search of the "ethnic vote," there have been some "multicultural programs" funded in the Southwest. Yet these programs, as honest as the people may be who are running them, can hardly be considered a serious attempt on the part of the U.S. government to restore the language and culture of the region.

The same general pattern exists with regard to the other captive nations within the U.S. as well as within nations outside the territorial U.S. that are subject to U.S. imperialism—nations such as Guatemala or "South" Korea for example. The dominant practice in schools objectively and subjectively attacks nationhood. This serves the interest of the U.S. ruling class since that class depends for its profits on exploitation of the captive nations as well as on its own exploited workers.

In contradiction to that, it is in the interest both of the U.S. working class as a whole and of the oppressed national minorities within the U.S. to uphold and defend the rights of nations to self-determination. For educators, this entails a struggle against the dominant school practices—a struggle to restore the language and culture of captive nations, to restore awareness of boundaries, to teach the history of imperialist conquest, including the destruction of the indigenous economic base and the exploitation of natural resources and labor resources by U.S. monopoly capital. Here too, then, there is a contradiction with regard to control of knowledge, between the interest of the ruling class, the bourgeoisie, and the interest of the exploited and oppressed.

Historical Materialism

Historical materialism, as I said at the beginning of this chapter, is the science of dialectical materialism applied to the study of historical development. It should be contrasted both to mechanical analysis which locates the basis of change external to the phenomenon in question, and to idealism which locates the motive force of historical development in "ideals" held by individuals rather than in the concrete *material interest* of classes. As I pointed out in the section on ideology, the focus on ideals and on individuals serves the interest of the ruling class. Historical materialism, on the other hand, is the scientific tool that enables the oppressed masses to identify, understand, and act on behalf of their own interests.

Idealism and mechanical logic run all through the school curriculum both formally and informally, and practically nowhere are students taught to examine the material basis of action or the dialectical relations of things. Thus, there is a general contradiction in schools between mechanical and idealist explanation and analysis on the one hand, and historical materialism on the other. The first is overwhelmingly dominant and serves the interest of the bourgeoisie. The second is almost invisible, and would serve the interest of the exploited classes. (Though I have not studied this enough to be sure, I suspect that certain student behavior which is consistently rejected by teachers can be more adequately explained as manifesting dialectical and materialist thought than as manifesting the vaguer psychological phenomenon called "creativity.")

This general contradiction takes many specific forms. One such form is the treatment of the subject of politics in schools. In this area control of knowledge takes several forms, but the main form is omission. Despite the fact that leading theorists of capitalist "democracy" in general (like Thomas Jefferson) and of schools under capitalist "democracy" in particular (like Horace Mann) argue that the populace must be trained to participate in our country's political life, the study of politics is not a sustained part of the formal curriculum. The actual workings of the political system are shrouded in mystery under the rubric of the "neutrality" of schools, and what is presented at all is confined to the competition between different tactics and positions within capitalist "democracy."

The primary messages conveyed to students through what little study of politics does take place are: (a) that "we" all really want the same thing and have different ideas about how to get it;

and (b) that progress results primarily from the ideals of leaders rather than from the life and death struggle between the contradictory interests of different classes in society. Political positions or thoughts or acts that suggest something contrary to these two propositions are rarely examined in schools. When they are examined at all, they are either distorted in such a way that the contradiction between them and the official bourgeoisie view of politics is obscured, or they are treated in a blatantly dishonest pejorative way, treated as "un-American" (as if the interests of "American" and the interest of the U.S. ruling class were synonymous) or as a ploy on the part of power-hungry fanatics. In short, omission, confusion, and mystification are the chief means of control of political knowledge practiced by the schools in the interest of the ruling class. Just beneath the surface of the political phenomena that are studied is one unrelenting fact that the ruling class is committed to keeping obscured, and which most people know anyway, but are denied the chance to study systematically: the fact that every political act represents the material interest of a class, and conversely, that the material interest of any class is promoted through class struggle. The study of politics, if it is to serve the interest of the ruling class, must not lead to systematic knowledge of these facts.

The contradiction here is obvious. Understanding of politics in the light of historical materialism and skill at dialectical analysis of political situations would provide the exploited classes with the theoretical basis for a successful struggle to end their exploitation by overturning the rule of capital.

Health, Technology, and Science

Is it not remarkable that a technologically advanced country like the United States, with a long history of compulsory "education," has not taught any but a handful of its people the rudiments of community health? Is it oversight that explains why we are "experimenting" with terminal syphilis on jailed subjects while a "backward" country like China eliminated syphilis entirely in a two-year program relying chiefly on volunteer paramedical personnel—a program that Western-trained doctors said could never work? Is there something to be learned from the fact that millions of working-class families go into debt annually to replace or have repaired household machinery that any high school student could repair, with a little training, at practically no cost?

One of the characteristics of technologically advanced capitalist countries is the development of a vast sector of the petty bourgeoisie administering the production of profit for the ruling class. To be brief about a very simple matter, one of the functions of this class is to keep in the hands of profit-producing enterprises the scientific knowledge needed to maintain certain aspects of daily life. As recent investigations by Senator Clark are revealing, for example, the medical clique uses the full weight of its prestige to destroy the reputation of doctors who try to break the near-monopoly control of medical services in order to bring health to patients who cannot afford doctors or medicine.[7]

The medical business is among the most lucrative. Profits in the pharmaceutical industry are as high as in oil or in automobile manufacture. And in the field of simple household machinery, profits are augmented by deliberately rapid obsolescence, and obsolescence is dependent upon the owner's being mystified by the machine. Likewise, the hegemony of certain industries like the power industries depends upon people knowing so little about simple things that they are mystified into leaving political decisions that automatically affect their lives up to the technocratic elite.

Science is treated in schools in a way that supports this technocratic structure by producing ignorance on the one hand and the ideological underpinning for reliance on an elite on the other. First, scientific subjects themselves are available only to an academic elite through the tracking system. Second, the subject matter of science instruction is geared to the structure of elite academic discipline which in turn is geared to profit maximization rather than to perceived social needs. This is doubly destructive in that on the one hand it discourages students whose primary concerns are social from taking science courses, while on the other hand it blinds developing scientists to the fact that ultimately the overall direction of science is determined by social forces in the interest of the bourgeoisie.[8] Third, by making the only route to such courses as community health work dependent upon completion of an academically arduous and elite course of study, the bourgeoisie engenders the notion that the only people who can provide certain services are the elite. Fourth, by treating science courses as more

---

[7] The results of Senator Clark's investigations are available in: *The Congressional Record.*

[8] Bourgeoisie = ruling class. The bourgeoisie is the class that owns the means of production. In a society in which law is based upon property, the class that owns the means of production is necessarily the ruling class.

appropriate to men than to women, the bourgeoisie creates a dependency on the part of women, who are most directly in touch with family health and nutrition and most in need of well-functioning household machinery. Fifth, conversely to the above four items, the schools fail to provide the masses of students with concrete knowledge of a nonacademic nature that would enable them to attend to routine health, nutritional, and technological problems faced every day without reliance on immense profit-making bureaucracies.

The direct contradiction between class interests is perhaps clearer in this area than in the others I have discussed because it involves such direct abuse of knowledge in pursuit of profit. Yet the most important point is not the direct exploitation I have just described. The important point is that people with technical skill are increasingly owned by the ruling class and that the schools' system for teaching science assures that this will continue to be the case. Consequently, all political decisions that depend upon or can be made to appear to depend upon technological knowledge are easily co-opted by the ruling class. This constitutes a direct attack on the political rights that the masses do have under capitalist democracy. The more political problems are wrapped in the mystique of technical talk, the easier it becomes for the ruling class to disguise its interests while it concentrates political decisions in its own hands.

This brief discussion is sufficient, perhaps, to show how the class struggle, the contradiction between the interests of the ruling class and the exploited classes, manifests itself in schools in the form of control of knowledge.

Training of the Labor Force

Liberal intellectuals are forever lamenting the fact that school is so much like a factory. Though the comparison contains some truth, the lament is false because it is based, on the one hand, on a combination of elitism toward the working class and ignorance of the actual social significance of the factory mode of production and, on the other hand, on a wholly romantic and objectively reactionary notion of the "freedom" that children "should" enjoy. Liberal intellectuals see in factory work only the loss of individual freedom. True to their assigned role in capitalist society, and acting as if "individual freedom" existed in U.S. society except for its accidental abrogation in factory and school, they set themselves the task of reforming, or as it is fashionable to say these days, "humanizing" the schools to make them more consonant with the "American" way.

Reflecting their class outlook and their training, their analysis is mechanical. Liberal intellectuals understand neither the dialectics of the factory nor the dialectics of freedom. Consequently, while they are right that school is in some respects like a factory, their comparison has illuminated neither and their lament has changed neither.

Engels pointed out that under capitalism, the mode of production is socialized while the ownership and consequently the appropriation of the value produced are not.[9] This is the central contradiction in the factory, and it must be understood if the comparison of school to factory is to teach us anything.

Prior to capitalism, most production took place on an individual basis, and some production took place on the basis of small groups working cooperatively at handcrafts. These modes of production are limited as to output, and two things had to occur to move to a more advanced mode of production. First, the technology had to develop that would allow the construction of the machinery needed to concentrate the work force in mass production units. Second, individuals had to accumulate the capital necessary to build the units of mass production. These two conditions matured slowly over a long period of time. As they did, the comparative efficiency of mass production enabled the capitalists to force an increasing number of workers out of individual modes of production and into concentrated modes, that is, into factories.

The very heart of the factory system is the concentration of labor it entails. Yet concentration does not mean simply bringing a large number of workers to a single place to do precisely what they used to do miles apart. It means socializing the productive process, coordinating a large number of different labor operations into a single unified stream of production. By definition, the labor force in a given factory is objectively a highly socialized unit. Also, objectively, it is an exploited unit—its labor power is purchased by the capitalists and the value it creates as a socialized unit is appropriated by the owners. This situation creates the central contradiction in the factory mode of production. On the one hand, because it is objectively socialized, the labor force creates enormous wealth in comparison to what it created on the basis of individual production. On the other hand, because they are forced to sell their labor power and because the great wealth they produce is appropriated by the owners, the workers are deprived of the wealth they produce. This is the meaning of the contradiction between labor and capital.

[9] See: Friedrich Engels. *Socialism: Utopian and Scientific*, Part III. New York: International Publishers Company, 1935.

The problem this contradiction creates for capitalists is that in creating the force that makes them wealthy they have also created the force that can (and will) destroy them. And the basis for any kind of freedom for the masses of workers that is anything more than a vicious fraud is freedom from exploitation at the hands of the capitalists. In this situation, the basic tactic of the bourgeoisie is to prevent the objective situation of the working class from becoming its subjective situation; to maintain the working class as a class *in* itself while preventing it from becoming a class *for* itself—while preventing it from becoming fully class conscious.

Michael Katz reports upon a correspondence in 1841 from some manufacturers to Horace Mann and George Boutwell, who were both involved in the founding of our "public" school system:

> One wrote that knowledge was secondary to morality, and that educated workers showed "more orderly and respectful . . . deportment," plus a greater willingness "to comply with the . . . regulations of an establishment." During labor disputes, the same experienced capitalist wrote, "I have always looked to the most intelligent, best educated, and the most moral for support." It goes without saying that it was "the ignorant and uneducated . . . the most turbulent and troublesome" who acted "under the impulse of excited passion and jealousy." The association of virtues was significant: Education, morality, and docility were all equated; they formed a trinity marking a properly schooled man. If there be any doubt on that point, consider the words of another manufacturer, who praised the "diligence and . . . willing acquiescence" of the educated who, working their way into the confidence of their colleagues, exerted "a conservative influence" in times of labor trouble, an influence "of good value pecuniarily and morally." The common school made company men.[10]

A laborer who is a "company man" is precisely a laborer who subjectively denies that the working class is a class *for* itself and who objectively helps the company maintain labor as a class *in* itself and *for* the company.

Thus, Katz's manufacturers provide us with the concrete basis of the comparison between the factory and the school. The interest of the bourgeoisie is to use the schools to train a labor force that will act as a class *in* itself but not as a class *for* itself. In contradiction to this, the interest of the working class is to become a class for itself.

The school contains the same contradiction the factory does. The school has the function of training an objectively socialized work force, and in school students *are* objectively a highly socialized

---

[10] Michael Katz. *Class, Bureaucracy, and Schools.* New York: Praeger Publishers, 1971. Copyright © 1971, Praeger Publishers.

work force. Their future exploitation depends upon their learning to accept their objective condition without becoming subjectively aware of it as the basis for turning the system around to serve their own interests. The interest of the student parallels the interest of the working class in becoming class conscious, in becoming a class for itself.

Thus, the social situation of workers and the social situation of students contain the same fundamental contradiction. Thus, school administrators are faced with the same problem as factory managers—how to exploit the social situation without allowing a class conscious analysis to develop among the exploited.

Schools achieve this through a number of means. The most direct is the almost universal taboo upon making the school itself an object of study. For example, the function of keeping curriculum out of the hands of students is not that it prevents bad decisions, but that it forestalls the necessity of students actually studying the institution they are compelled to attend. As a teacher at various levels, I have often sought to direct students into study of the school or the classroom they were in, and I have found each time that this step, more than any other so-called radical step makes administrators fearful. And the things I see as most advantageous are precisely the things they fear the most.

For example, the greatest pedagogical advantage is that the school or classroom itself is the only available social object about which it is logistically possible for students to develop any kind of consistent and sustained dialectical unity of theory and practice. It is the only available social object about which students can explore in a sustained way the dialectical unity of analysis and purpose expressed as action. It is the only available social object about which students can investigate the dialectical relation between interest and ideology expressed as educational practice. These inquiries are neither too difficult for nor ungermane to the maturation of young students. Yet they do directly violate the strictures on studying the immediate oppressive social situation.

This taboo calls attention to another way the school opposes class consciousness, for the taboo entails not only a restriction of subject matter, but also a restriction of method. Each of the pedagogical strengths I referred to is a strength because it involves a dialectical rather than a mechanical method.

While the *basis* for class consciousness is the contradiction between labor and capital, a necessary *condition* for it is *dialectical* analysis which illuminates contradictions in a situation. An important postulate of Marxism is that class consciousness does not arise "spontaneously" in the class struggle. It requires the introduction of the theory and methods of dialectical materialism. Thus, restrictions upon the introduction of dialectical materialist analysis in schools have the effect of inhibiting the growth of class consciousness. And conversely, the growth of class consciousness would be greatly facilitated if students were taught the dialectical method of looking at social situations in general and their school situation in particular. The contradiction between the dialectical materialist and mechanical, idealist, or metaphysical methods of analysis is an aspect in schools of the contradiction between labor and capital. Not only is the dialectical method opposed through opposition to educational projects that would entail its use; not only does the "public" school not teach dialectical theory and method; it reflects in its structures and methods, and thereby conveys to the students, an antidialectical, a metaphysical view of social problems.

The basic characteristic of the schools' metaphysical analysis is the substitution of metaphysical polarities for dialectical materialist unities. Thus, the problem of the individual is represented as individual uniqueness vs. group conformity, and the problem of authority is represented as institutional authority vs. personal freedom. Posing problems this way both reflects and reinforces metaphysical thinking by locking each question into a hopelessly static standoff between two idealist camps favoring two opposing "ideals" on a priori metaphysical grounds. A direct consequence of this kind of analysis of social problems is the reduction of disagreement to total subjectivism. For example, the official position of the school is that in social or political matters each person is entitled to his or her own opinion, and no view can ever be anything more than a subjective opinion. On the liberal side, this results in nonsense like "value clarification" procedures which individualize interests, reduce interests to "opinions," and isolate opinion on the one side from knowledge and on the other side from action. On the conservative side, it legitimizes the arbitrary exercise of authority by releasing the authorities from the obligation to justify their "opinions." They are free, even obliged, to exercise their authority on behalf of what they think is "best for all concerned."

On the one hand, then, the pervasive metaphysical analysis teaches students: that social and political views are matters of individual opinion rather than of class interest; that social and political views are based on subjectivity and are not amenable to objective study or scientific analysis. Therefore, no view is any more correct than any other. Politics thus becomes indistinguishable from gastronomy—*de gustibus non est disputandum.*

And, on the other hand, that authority is its own justification.

Recalling that the problem facing school administrators as instrumentalities of the bourgeoisie is "how to exploit the social situation without allowing a class conscious analysis to develop among the exploited," it is not difficult to see how their characteristically metaphysical analysis of social problems serves their interests.

A dialectical materialist analysis of the same problems teaches something very different. There is no meaning to *categories* like individual, group, freedom, and authority. These are contradictory aspects of a social unity. The key question in the application of a dialectical materialist analysis is the question "for whom?" The relation between the individual and group is determined not by juggling metaphysical categories, but rather by examining material interests.

In a society based on class structure and the exploitation by one class of other classes, the relation of individual to group is determined by class relationships. For members of the working class, each person is objectively a member of the class. The class exists in itself as an objective reality. It is in the interest of all members of the class to develop consciousness of the unity of their individual interests and the interests of their class; the development of this consciousness in each individual is the basis for the transformation of the working class from a class *in* itself to a class *for* itself. Whereas in the contradiction between labor and capital the primary factor is struggle, in the contradiction between individual and class, the primary factor is unity; and thus the contradiction between the individual and the class is resolved by the development of collectivity. The unity of the individual and the class is not the same thing as conformity. Conformity to the class is the basis for exploitation, a mere reinforcement of its character as existing *in* itself. Opposing metaphysical individualism to conformity only sustains the objective existence of the class *in* itself. Collectivity, the unity of individual and class, is the basis for resisting exploitation because it represents the development of class consciousness.

Thus, whereas metaphysical analysis leads only to a hollow and motionless standoff between categories which inhibits the growth of class consciousness and thereby operates in the interest of the bourgeoisie, dialectical materialism provides a dynamic analysis pointing toward a resolution of the contradiction that fosters the growth of class consciousness and thereby carries forward the interest of the exploited classes.

The same is true with regard to the problem of authority and freedom. As with the problem of the individual, the starting point in a dialectical materialist analysis of freedom and authority is the question "for whom?" In a society divided into exploiting and exploited, ruling and ruled classes, there can be no meaning attached to "freedom in general," and no meaning attached to "freedom from authority." The ruling class has relative "freedom" by virtue of the authority it exercises over the classes it exploits. For the exploited classes, there is only as much "freedom" as the ruling class deems consistent with its own interests at a given stage in the development of capitalism. For the exploited, this means a certain amount of political freedom in exchange for absolute economic submission. To talk about freedom in general is to deny the existence of classes and the history of class struggle. For the educator, to talk about freedom for children without reference to the class struggle is to blind oneself to the economic and political reality the child lives in and will live in and to leave the child helpless in the face of that reality.

"Freedom" is meaningful, in class society, only as the struggle for an end to exploitation by one class of the masses. This struggle is class struggle of the exploited and oppressed against the ruling class. It has certain fixed historical features, and is guided by analysis of these features. Participation in the struggle thus imposes upon each person the requirement that he or she submit to the authority of those historical features, to the authority of the interest of the exploited classes, to the authority of the historical situation of the class struggle. Thus, through dialectical materialism, through a dialectical analysis of the relation of freedom to authority in light of material class interest, the contradiction between freedom and authority is resolved. Their unity lies in struggle against the ruling class. Their unity, therefore, entails the growth of class consciousness. Teaching a dialectical analysis of freedom and authority entails the teaching of class consciousness. Thus, I can repeat the conclusion I drew from analyzing the relation between individual and group; whereas, metaphysical analysis leads to a standoff that undermines the growth of class consciousness and thus serves the interest of the bourgeoisie, dialectical materialism provides a resolution of the contradiction that carries forward the growth of class consciousness and thus serves the interest of the exploited classes.

The metaphysical analysis pervades the school. Its basis is in the material interests of the bourgeoisie; it is expressed concretely in those structures and methods of schooling that have to do with the treatment of individuals and groups, the treatment of authority and freedom, etc.; as part of the "tacit curriculum" it is explicitly taught to the students; it concretely militates against the growth of class consciousness; and finally, the growth of class consciousness would be facilitated if dialectical materialist analysis pervaded the school, if the structures and methods expressed this analysis, if the students were thereby, through the tacit curriculum, taught to analyze social problems with the tools of dialectical materialism.

In summary, our concern, in this chapter and throughout the book, with "contradictions" is not a new gimmick. It entails the systematic use of the tools of dialectical materialism.

Contradictions in the schools reflect the fundamental contradictions in capitalist society, and the root contradiction is the class contradiction—the contradiction between labor and capital. Schools cannot be understood apart from a class analysis of society. They are an instrument of class struggle, and they serve the interest of the ruling class.

The contradiction between the interest of the ruling class and the interest of the exploited masses appears principally in three forms: control of ideology, control of knowledge, and training of the work force.

Control of ideology entails falsification of the history, meaning, and concrete status of democracy. By presenting U.S. democracy as the product of idealist philosophy rather than as the product of the emergence of certain economic interests, the schools buttress the institutions of the bourgeoisie against attack. By presenting U.S. democracy as "pure" democracy rather than as relative class democracy, the schools protect the bourgeoisie itself against attack.

Control of knowledge entails depriving the masses of certain categories of concrete knowledge the possession of which would enormously strengthen them in their struggle for democracy and against exploitation. With regard to history, the contradiction between labor and capital takes the form of suppression of the history of class struggle. With regard to national minorities, it takes the form of suppression of both the objective and subjective factors that are the basis of the struggle for national liberation—namely: territory, culture, economic basis, language, and psychological makeup. With regard to health, science, and technology, it takes the form of suppression of:

1. The knowledge people need to free themselves of economic exploitation at the hands of the technocratic servants of capital, and

2. The knowledge people need to combat the co-optation of political decisions by the capitalists through their technocratic bureaucracy.

Training of the work force is the area in which the contradiction between labor and capital manifests itself in schools in the most direct form. The interest of the bourgeoisie is advanced by maintaining the work force as an objectively socialized class *in* itself while prohibiting its maturation into a subjectively conscious class *for* itself. Schools train students to operate as an objectively socialized work force, and employ a number of strategies for combatting the development of class consciousness: by prohibiting or severely restricting study of the institution itself, which also undermines any serious engagement on the part of students to participate in planning their own education; by excluding from its program the study and use of the dialectical materialist method of analysis; by teaching, through structures and methods that constitute the schools' tacit curriculum, a metaphysical analysis of social problems instead of a dialectical materialist analysis which would lead directly to the growth of class consciousness.

In conclusion, the contradiction between the interest of the ruling class and the interest of the exploited and oppressed classes and peoples is manifested in a number of ways in the "public" schools. The interest of the bourgeoisie clearly dominates the schools, and this can be seen in the way their interest controls ideology, knowledge, and the training of the work force. The tasks of progressive educators are (a) to devise and put into practice tactics that will undermine bourgeois domination in these areas, and (b) to strive in every possible way, including the organization of student, teacher, parent, and community groups, for educational programs that will serve the oppressed and exploited masses by equipping them concretely with the knowledge and skills they need to carry forward the class struggle.

6. Commonsense Categories and Curriculum Thought*

Michael W. Apple

"There's the King's messenger," said the Queen. "He's in prison now, being punished; and the trial doesn't even begin 'til next Wednesday; and of course the crime comes last of all."

"Suppose he never commits the crime?" said Alice.

"That would be all the better, wouldn't it?" the Queen said, as she turned the plaster round her finger with a bit of ribbon.

Alice felt there was no denying *that*. "Of course it would be all the better," she said, "but it wouldn't be all the better his being punished."

"You're wrong *there*, at any rate," said the Queen. "Were you ever punished?"

"Only for faults," said Alice.

"And you were all the better for it, I know!" the Queen said triumphantly.

"Yes, but then I *had* done the things I was punished for," said Alice, "that makes all the difference."

"But if you hadn't done them," the Queen said, "that would have been better still; better, and better, and better!"—Lewis Carroll, *Through the Looking Glass*

MY ORIENTATION HERE will be to explore critically certain aspects of social institutions—particularly the school—and our ways of talking about and engaging in research about them. This will be done with a view toward building the sort of perspective and forms

* A briefer version of portions of this essay was presented at the conference, "Toward the Reconstruction of the Curriculum Field," Philadelphia, Pennsylvania, May 10-11, 1973.

of knowledge that will enable educators to construct more just institutions of schooling.

I am particularly interested in exploring the ethical dimensions of our accepted ways of viewing students. Educational questions are, at least partly, moral questions. For one thing they assume choices as to the relevant realms of expertise educators should use to comprehend children and schools. As Blum puts it, "All inquiry [and especially educational inquiry I might add] displays a moral commitment in that it makes reference to an authoritative election concerning how a phenomenon ought to be understood." [1] Furthermore, if conceptions of "the moral" concern questions of oughtness or goodness, then it should be clear that educational questions are moral questions on this criterion as well. Finally, by the very fact that school people influence students, their acts cannot be interpreted fully without the use of an ethical rubric.

However, there are a number of factors that cause educators to perceive their problems in ways significantly different from this. Because this causal nexus is exceptionally complex, this paper cannot hope to explore all aspects of the difficulty. To do so would require an extensive investigation of the relationship between science, ideology, and educational thought [2] and an analysis of the reduction of conceptions of humans and institutions to technical considerations in advanced industrial societies.[3] Hopefully, this essay will serve as a stimulus for further inquiry into these areas and especially into the ways by which school people pass over the ethical and, as we shall see, political implications of their acts.

The investigation to be sketched out in what follows is theoretic. However, its implications for the day to day density of classroom life are exceptionally important. I am using the idea of a theoretic investigation in a rather specific way in this analysis. I wish to begin to explore ways of illuminating some of the taken-for-granted or commonsense assumptions which underpin the curriculum field.

---

[1] Alan F. Blum. "Sociology, Wrongdoing, and Akrasia: An Attempt To Think Greek about the Problem of Theory and Practice." In: Robert A. Scott and Jack D. Douglas, editors. *Theoretical Perspectives on Deviance.* New York: Basic Books, Inc., Publishers, 1972. p. 343. Copyright © 1972 by Robert A. Scott and Jack D. Douglas.

[2] See: Jürgen Habermas. *Knowledge and Human Interests.* Boston: Beacon Press, 1971; and Peter Berger and Thomas Luckmann. *The Social Construction of Reality.* New York: Doubleday & Company, 1966.

[3] See, for example: Hannah Arendt. *The Human Condition.* New York: Doubleday & Company, 1958; and Albrecht Wellmer. *Critical Theory of Society.* New York: Herder & Herder, 1971.

This type of orientation has been noted most clearly by Douglas in his statement concerning the differences between a naturalistic and a theoretical stance. He puts it this way:

> There are different ways to make use of commonsense experience. . . . There is, especially, a fundamental distinction between taking the *natural* (or *naturalistic*) stance and taking the *theoretic* stance, as the phenomenological philosophers have long called them. Taking the natural stance consists primarily in *taking the standpoint of common sense*, of *acting within* common sense, whereas taking the theoretic stance consists in *standing back from common sense* and *studying common sense to determine its nature*.[4]

That is, for Douglas and myself, one must bracket any commitment to the utility of employing our taken-for-granted perspectives so that these commonsense presuppositions themselves can become subject to investigation. In this way our commonsense presuppositions can be used as *data* to focus upon the latent significance of much that we unquestioningly do in schools. This is particularly important because they provide the basic logic which organizes our activity and often act as tacit guidelines for determining the success or failure of our educational procedures.

It is not the case, however, that these ideological configurations have been constructed consciously. The very fact that they have grown from commonsense presuppositions makes them even more difficult to deal with. They are difficult to question, that is, because they rest upon assumptions that are unarticulated and that seem essential in making some headway in education. But other things contribute to the lack of critical insight. In the field of education these configurations are academically and socially respectable and are supported by the prestige of a process that "shows every sign of being valid scholarship, complete with tables of numbers, copious footnotes, and scientific terminology." Furthermore, the altruistic and humanitarian elements of these positions are quite evident, so it is hard to conceive of them as principally functioning to detract from our ability to solve social or educational problems.[5]

However, an investigation into the history of many ameliorative reform movements that were supported by research and perspectives similar to those we will consider here documents the rather interesting fact that often the ameliorative reforms had quite problematic

---

[4] Jack D. Douglas. *American Social Order*. New York: The Free Press, 1971. pp. 9-10. Douglas' stress.

[5] William Ryan. *Blaming the Victim*. New York: Random House, Inc., 1971. pp. 21-22.

results. Frequently they ultimately even ended up harming the individuals upon whom they focused. Platt's treatment of the reform of the juvenile justice system in the latter part of the last century is instructive here.

In attempting to create more humane conditions for "wayward" youth, these reforms created a new category of deviance called "juvenile delinquency" and in the long run served to abridge the civil and constitutional rights of youth.[6] In many ways, we have yet to recover from these "reforms." As I shall argue in this paper, many of the seemingly ameliorative reforms school people propose in schools, and the assumptions that lie behind them, have the same effect—ultimately harming rather than helping, clouding over basic issues and value conflicts rather than contributing to our ability to face them honestly.

This is especially the case in the major topic of this paper, the process of using clinical, psychological, and therapeutic perspectives and labels in schools. These forms of language and the perspectives they embody may be interpreted not as "helping," but more critically as a mechanism by which schools engage in anonymizing and sorting out individuals into preordained social, economic, and educational slots.

The labeling process, thus, tends to function as a form of social control,[7] a "worthy" successor to a long line of mechanisms in schools that sought to homogenize social reality, to eliminate disparate perceptions, and to use supposedly therapeutic means to create moral, valuative, and intellectual consensus.[8] The fact that this process can be deadening, that it results in the elimination of diversity, that it ignores the importance of conflict and surprise in human interaction is too often lost in the background in our rush to "help."

There is nothing very odd about the fact that we usually do not focus on the basic sets of assumptions which we use. First, they are normally known only tacitly, remain unspoken, and are very difficult to formulate explicitly. Second, these basic rules are so

[6] Anthony Platt. *The Child Savers: The Invention of Delinquency.* Chicago: University of Chicago Press, 1969.

[7] Edwin M. Schur. *Labeling Deviant Behavior.* New York: Harper & Row, Publishers, 1971. p. 33.

[8] On the dominance of a social control ethic in schools see: Clarence Karier, Paul Violas, and Joel Spring. *Roots of Crisis.* Chicago: Rand McNally & Co., 1973; and Barry Franklin. "The Curriculum Field and the Problem of Social Control, 1918-1938: A Study in Critical Theory." Unpublished doctoral thesis. University of Wisconsin, Madison, 1974.

much a part of us that they do not have to be expressed. By the very fact that they are *shared* assumptions, the product of specific groups of people, and are commonly accepted by most educators (if not most people in general), they only become problematic when an individual violates them [9] or else when a previously routine situation becomes significantly altered. However, if we are to be true to the demands of rigorous analysis, it is a critical inquiry into just such things as the routine grounds of our day to day experience that is demanded.

On the Necessity of Critical Awareness

The curriculum field, and education as a whole, has been quite ameliorative in its orientation. This is understandable given the pressures on and interest by the field to serve schools and their ongoing programs and concerns. The marked absorption in amelioration, however, has had some rather detrimental effects. Not only has it caused us to ignore questions and research that might contribute in the long run to our basic understanding of the process of schooling,[10] but such an orientation neglects the crucial role critical reflection must play if a field is to remain vital.

A critically reflective mode is important for a number of reasons. First, curriculum specialists help establish and maintain institutions that affect students and others in a myriad of ways. Because of these effects, they must be aware of the reasons and intentions that guide them. This is especially true of ideological and political purposes, both manifest and latent.[11] Since schools as institutions are so interconnected with other political and economic institutions which dominate a collectivity and since schools

[9] Douglas, *op. cit.,* p. 181. I have explored one of these *basic* or, as I have called them, *constitutive* rules—that of consensus—elsewhere. See: Michael W. Apple. "The Hidden Curriculum and the Nature of Conflict." *Interchange* 2 (4): 27-40; 1971. See also the discussion of interpretive and normative rules in: Aaron Cicourel. "Basic and Normative Rules in the Negotiation of Status and Role." Hans Peter Dreitzel, editor. *Recent Sociology, No. 2.* New York: The Macmillan Company, 1971. pp. 4-45.

[10] Herbert M. Kliebard. "Persistent Curriculum Issues in Historical Perspective." In: Edmund C. Short, editor. *The Search for Valid Content for Curriculum Courses.* Toledo: The University of Toledo, 1970. p. 33.

[11] I am using the concept of ideology here to refer to commonsense views of the world held by specific groups, not merely as "politically" biased views. This follows from Harris' statement that "Ideologies are not disguised descriptions of the world, but rather real descriptions of the world from a specific viewpoint, just as all descriptions of the world are from a particular viewpoint." See: Nigel Harris. *Beliefs in Society: The Problem of Ideology.* London: A. Watts and Co., 1968. p. 22.

often unquestioningly act to distribute knowledge and values through both the overt and hidden curricula that often act to support these same institutions, it is a necessity for educators to engage in searching analyses of the ways in which they allow values and commitments unconsciously to work through them.

Second, it is important to argue that the very activity of rational investigation requires a critical style. The curriculum field has been much too accepting of forms of thought that do not do justice to the complexity of inquiry and thus the field has not really changed its basic perspective for decades. It has been taken with the notions of systematicity, certainty, and control as the ideals of programmatic and conceptual activity, in its treatment of research and people. This is strongly mirrored in the behavioral objectives movement and in the quest for taxonomies which codify "cognitive," "affective," and "psychomotor" behavior. These activities find their basis in a conception of rationality that is less than efficacious today. Not only is it somewhat limiting,[12] but it also is historically and empirically inaccurate.

Our taken-for-granted view posits a conception of rationality based upon ordering beliefs and concepts in tidy logical structures and upon the extant intellectual paradigms which seem to dominate the field of curriculum at a given time. Yet, any serious conception of rationality must be concerned not with the specific intellectual positions a professional group or individual employs at any given time, but instead *with the conditions on which and the manner in which this field of study is prepared to criticize and change those accepted doctrines.*[13] In this way, intellectual flux, not "intellectual immutability," is the expected and normal occurrence. What has to be explained is *not* why we should change our basic conceptual structure, but rather the stability or crystallization of the forms of thought a field has employed over time.[14]

The crystallization and lack of change of fundamental perspectives is not a new problem in the curriculum field by any means. In fact, a major effort was made in the 1940's [15] to identify and deal

[12] See Susanne Langer's articulate treatment of the necessity of discursive *and* nondiscursive forms of rationality in her *Philosophy in a New Key.* New York: Mentor Books, 1951.

[13] Stephen Toulmin. *Human Understanding: The Collective Use and Evolution of Concepts.* Princeton, New Jersey: Princeton University Press, 1972. p. 84.

[14] *Ibid.,* p. 96.

[15] Alice Miel. *Changing the Curriculum: A Social Process.* New York: D. Appleton-Century Co., 1946.

with just such a concern. The fact that many curriculum specialists are unaware of the very real traditions of grappling with the field's tendency toward hardening its positions obviously points to the necessity of greater attention being given to historical scholarship in the curriculum field.

This intellectual conservatism often coheres with a social conservatism as well. It is not the case that a critical perspective is "merely" important for illuminating the stagnation of the curriculum field. What is even more crucial is the fact that means must be found to illuminate the concrete ways in which the curriculum field supports the widespread interests in technical control of human activity, in rationalizing, manipulating, and bureaucratizing individual action, and in eliminating personal style and political diversity. These are interests that dominate advanced industrial societies and they contribute quite a bit to the suffering of minorities and women, the alienation of youth, the malaise and meaninglessness of work for a large proportion of the population, and the increasing sense of powerlessness and cynicism that seems to dominate our society. Curriculum specialists and other educators need to be aware of all of these outcomes, yet there is little in-depth analysis of the role our commonsense thought plays in causing us to be relatively impotent in the face of these problems.

Many educators consistently attempt to portray themselves as being "scientific," by referring to the "scientific" (or technical) and therefore neutral status of their activity to give it legitimacy. They are thereby ignoring the fact that a good deal of social science research is currently being strongly criticized for its support of bureaucratized assumptions and institutions that deny dignity and significant choice to individuals and groups of people. This criticism cannot be shunted aside easily by educators, for unlike many other people, their activity has a direct influence on the present and future of masses of children. By being the primary institution through which individuals pass to become "competent" adults, schools give children no choice about the means by which they are distributed into certain roles in society. As we shall see, "neutral scientific" terminology acts as a veneer to cover this fact, and, thus, becomes more ideological than helpful.[16]

---

[16] Michael W. Apple. "The Process and Ideology of Valuing in Educational Settings." Michael W. Apple, Michael J. Subkoviak, and Henry S. Lufler, Jr., editors. *Educational Evaluation: Analysis and Responsibility.* Berkeley, California: McCutchan Publishing Corporation, 1974.

Perhaps one of the fundamental reasons the field has stagnated both socially and intellectually involves our lack of concern for less positivistic scholarship. We have been less than open to forms of analysis that would effectively counterbalance our use of rubrics embodying the interests of technical control and certainty. This lack of openness has caused us to be inattentive to the functions of the very language systems we employ and has led us to disregard fields whose potency lies in their concern for a critical perspective. This will require a closer examination.

Are Things As They Seem?

Let us focus first on the linguistic tools we employ to talk about "students" in schools. My basic point will be that much of our language, while seemingly neutral, is not neutral in its impact nor is it unbiased in regard to existing institutions of schooling. An underlying thesis of this argument, and one which can only be treated in less depth than it merits, is that our accepted faith that the extension of "neutral techniques of science and technology" will provide solutions to all of the dilemmas we confront is misplaced and that such a faith tends to obscure the fact that much of educational research serves and justifies already existing technical control systems that accept the distribution of power in American society as given.[17] Much of the discussion here will be stimulated by the insights derived from recent reconstructed Marxist scholarship, particularly the potent notion that our basic perspectives often hide our "real" relationships with other persons with whom we have real and symbolic contact. The analysis will employ arguments from research on the process of labeling to bring this initial point home.

Before proceeding, it would be wise to examine some possible explanations of why critical Marxist understanding has had less than a major impact on our commonsense thought. This is odd since it is considered exceptionally powerful in other fields and on the European continent where, for example, it has made quite an impact on French and German philosophical and sociological thought.[18]

[17] Such a statement obviously needs justification, more than is possible in a paper of this length. Provocative and insightful discussions of the problem can be found in: Trent Schroyer. "Toward a Critical Theory for Advanced Industrial Society." In: Hans Peter Dreitzel, editor. *Recent Sociology, No. 2.* New York: The Macmillan Company, 1970. pp. 210-34; and: Alvin W. Gouldner. *The Coming Crisis of Western Sociology.* New York: Basic Books, Inc., 1970.

[18] See: Jean-Paul Sartre. *Search for a Method.* New York: Vintage Books, 1963.

There are a number of reasons why reconstructed Marxist scholarship has not found a serious place in Anglo-Western educational investigation. While, historically, orthodox Marxism had an effect in the 1930's on such educators as Brameld, Counts, and others, the movement lost its potency due to the political situation evolving later.

To this problem, of course, can be added the overly deterministic and dogmatic interpretations of applying Marxist analysis by even many later "Marxists." Part of the problem of applying critical insights to advanced industrial societies like our own is to free these insights from their embeddedness in such dogmatism.[19] It should not have to be said, but unfortunately it must, that the rigidly controlled nature of a number of modern societies bears little relation to the uniquely cogent analyses found in the Marxist tradition itself. Our neglect of this scholarly tradition says more about the fear laden past of American society than it does about the merits of the (all too often unexplored) tradition of critical analysis.

Yet, there are other more basic and less overtly political explanations for the atrophy and lack of acceptance of a Marxist intellectual tradition in places like the United States. The atomistic and strict empiricist frame of mind so prevalent in our thought has difficulty with the critically oriented notion of the necessity of a plurality of ways of looking at the world. On this, critical scholarship holds a position quite similar to that of phenomenology in that the "truth" of something can only be seen through the use of the totality of perspectives one can bring to bear upon it.[20]

Also, the tendency in Western industrialized societies to strictly separate value from fact would make it difficult to accept a position which holds that most social and intellectual categories are themselves *valuative* in nature and may reflect ideological commitments, a fact that will be of exceptional import in this discussion. Furthermore, the long tradition of individualism and a strongly utilitarian frame of mind would no doubt cause one to look less than positively upon both a more social conception of man and an ideal commitment that is less apt to be immediately ameliorative and more apt to raise

[19] See, for example, the well written portrayal of Marx's own lack of rigid dogmatism in: Michael Harrington. *Socialism*. New York: Bantam Books, 1972. For a reappraisal of Marx's supposed economic determinism, one that argues against such an interpretation, see: Bertell Ollman. *Alienation: Marx's Conception of Man in Capitalist Society*. Cambridge: Cambridge University Press, 1971.

[20] Aron Gurwitsch. *The Field of Consciousness*. Pittsburgh: Duquesne University Press, 1964. p. 184.

basic questions about the very framework of social life that is accepted as given by a society.[21]

In opposition to the atomistic assumptions that predominate in our commensense thought, a critical viewpoint usually sees any object "relationally." This is an important key to understanding the type of analysis one might engage in from a reconstructed perspective. This implies two things. First, any subject matter under investigation must be seen in relation to its historical roots—how it evolved, from what conditions it arose—and its latent contradictions and tendencies in the future. In the highly complicated world of critical analysis, existing structures are actually in something like continual motion. Change and development are the norm and any institutional structure is "merely" a stage in process.[22] Thus, institutional reification becomes problematic, as do the patterns of thought that support this lack of institutional change. Second, anything being examined is defined not only by its obvious characteristics, but by its less overt ties to other factors. It *is* these ties or relationships that make the subject what it is and give it its primary meaning.[23] In this way, our ability to illuminate the interdependence and interaction of factors is considerably expanded.

To accept this relational view is obviously to go against our traditional concept that what we see is as it appears. In fact, the argument is that our very taken-for-granted perceptions mislead us here and that this is a rather grave limitation on our thought and action. That is, anything is a good deal more than it appears,[24] especially when one is dealing with complex and interrelated institutions including the school. It is this very point that will enable us to make progress in uncovering some of the functions of educational language.

One final point can be made. Historically, critical theory has been reduced to a variant of pragmatism, especially in the 30's by Sidney Hook and others. While I do not wish to debunk the pragmatic tradition in American education (after all, we still have much

[21] Charles Taylor. "Marxism and Empiricism." In: Bernard Williams and Alan Montifiore, editors. *British Analytic Philosophy.* New York: The Humanities Press, 1966. pp. 227-46.

[22] Bertell Ollman. *Alienation: Marx's Conception of Man in Capitalist Society.* Cambridge: Cambridge University Press, 1971. p. 18.

[23] *Ibid.*, p. 15. This position has been given the name of a "philosophy of internal relations." Oddly, such a view *has* had an extensive history of American thought, even somewhat in educational thought. See, for example, the work of Whitehead such as *Process and Reality.*

[24] *Ibid.*, p. 90.

to learn from a serious treatment of Dewey's analysis of means and ends in education, for instance), I do want to caution against interpreting critical analysis so that it easily fits within our taken-for-granted perspectives. To do so is to lose the potential of a critical perspective in going beyond some of the very real conformist inclinations of pragmatism.

The pragmatic position tends to ignore the possibility that some theories must contradict the present reality and, in fact, must consistently work against it.[25] These critical inquiries *stand in witness* of the negativity involved in all too many current institutional (economic, cultural, educational, political) arrangements and thus can illuminate the possibility of significant change. In this way, critical theory contributes to emancipation in that it shows the way linguistic or social institutions have been reified or "thingified" so that educators and the public at large have forgotten why they evolved, and that people made them and thus can change them.[26]

The intent of such a critique and of critical scholarship in general, then, is twofold. First, it aims at illuminating the tendencies for unwanted and often unconscious domination, alienation, and repression within certain existing cultural, political, educational, and economic institutions. Second, through exploring the negative effects and contradictions of much that unquestioningly goes on in these institutions, it seeks to "promote conscious emancipatory activity." [27] That is, it examines what is supposed to be happening in, say, schools, if one takes the language and slogans of many school people seriously; and, it then shows how these things *actually* work in a manner that is destructive of ethical rationality and personal political and institutional power. Once this actual functioning is held up to scrutiny, it attempts to point to concrete activity that will lead to challenging this taken-for-granted activity.

An example of some aspects of the approach we have been discussing might be an analysis of the major concepts and procedures which dominate educational activity today, with systems management offering a good instance. By linking this taken-for-granted procedure to its historical precedents and showing the latent tendencies within it, and at the same time exploring the relationships or ties that educational systems analysis has to a conservative institu-

---

[25] Martin Jay. *The Dialectical Imagination.* Boston: Little, Brown and Company, 1973. p. 83.

[26] *Ibid.,* p. 268.

[27] Trent Schroyer. *The Critique of Domination.* New York: George Braziller, 1973. pp. 30-31.

tional and ideological framework, hidden social and valuative commitments are made clear.[28] It may very well be the case that until such commitments are uncovered, the field of curriculum itself will make little headway in creating educational institutions that are humanly responsive. A similar instance involves the linguistic categories curriculum specialists and other educators employ to order, guide, and give meaning to their work.

Institutional Language and Ethical Responsibility

One of the most potent issues raised by critical scholarship over the years is the tendency for us to hide what are profound interrelations between persons through the use of a "neutral" commodity language.[29] That is, educators have developed categories and modes of perception which reify or "thingify" individuals so that they (the educators) can confront students as institutional abstractions rather than concrete persons. Given the complexity of mass education this is understandable. However, the implications of the growth of this form of language are profound and must be examined in depth.

In order to accomplish this, one fact must be made clear. The categories that curriculum workers and other educators employ are themselves social constructs. They also imply the notion of the power of one group to "impose" these social constructions on others. For example, the categories by which we differentiate "smart" from "stupid" children, "academic" from "nonacademic" areas, "play" from "learning" activity, and even "students" from "teachers," are all commonsense constructions *which grow out of the nature of existing institutions.*[30] As such they must be treated as historically conditioned data, not absolutes. This is not to say that they are necessarily wrong; rather it points to the necessity of understanding them for what they are—categories that developed out of specific social and historical situations which conform to a specific frame-

[28] See: Michael W. Apple. "The Adequacy of Systems Management Procedures in Education." In: Albert H. Yee, editor. *Perspectives on Management Systems Approaches in Education.* Englewood Cliffs, New Jersey: Educational Technology Press, 1973. pp. 3-31.

[29] Shlomo Avineri. *The Social and Political Thought of Karl Marx.* Cambridge: Cambridge University Press, 1968. p. 117. Avineri puts it this way, "Ultimately, a commodity is an objectified expression of an intersubjective relationship."

[30] Michael F. D. Young. "Introduction." In: Michael F. D. Young, editor. *Knowledge and Control.* London: Macmillan, 1971. p. 2.

work of assumptions and institutions, the use of which categories brings with it the logic of the institutional assumptions as well.

As I mentioned, the field itself has a tendency to "disguise" relations between people as relations between things or abstractions.[31] Hence, ethical issues such as the profoundly difficult problem concerning the ways by which one person may seek to influence another are not usually treated as important considerations. It is here that the abstract categories that grow out of institutional life become quite serious. If an educator may define another as a "slow learner," a "discipline problem," or other general category, he or she may prescribe general "treatments" that are seemingly neutral and helpful. However, by the very fact that the categories themselves are based upon institutionally defined abstractions (the commonsense equivalent of statistical averages), the educator is freed from the more difficult task of examining the institutional context that caused these abstract labels to be placed upon a concrete individual in the first place. Thus, the understandable attempt to reduce complexity leads to the use of "average treatments" applied to fillers of abstract roles. This preserves the anonymity of the intersubjective relationship between "educator" and "pupil" which is so essential if institutional definitions of situations are to prevail. It, thereby, protects both the existing institution and the educator from self-doubt and from the innocence and reality of the child.

This has important implications for educational scholarship. By using official categories and constructs such as those defined by and growing out of existing institutional practices—examples might be studies of the "slow learner," "discipline problems," and "remediation," curriculum researchers may be lending the rhetorical prestige of science to what may be questionable practices of an educational bureaucracy.[32] That is, there is no rigorous attempt to examine *institutional* culpability. The notion of imputing culpability is of considerable moment to our analysis. Scott makes this point rather clearly in his discussion of the effects of labeling someone as different or deviant.

Another reaction that commonly occurs when a deviant label is applied is that within the community a feeling arises that "something ought to be done about *him*." Perhaps the most important fact about this reaction in our society is that almost all of the steps that are taken are

---

[31] On the relationship between this transformation of human interaction into other reified forms and an ideological, political, and economic framework, see: Ollman, *op. cit.,* pp. 198-99.

[32] Douglas, *op. cit.,* pp. 70-71.

directed solely at the deviant. Punishment, rehabilitation, therapy, coercion, and other common mechanisms of social control are things that are done to him, implying that the causes of deviance reside within the person to whom the label has been attached, and that the solutions to the problems that he presents can be achieved by doing something to him. This is a curious fact, particularly when we examine it against the background of social science research on deviance that so clearly points to the crucial role played by ordinary people in determining who is labeled a deviant and how a deviant behaves. *This research suggests that none of the corrective measures that are taken can possibly succeed in the intended way unless they are directed at those who confer deviant labels as well as those to whom they are applied.*[33]

In clearer language, in the school students are the persons expressly focused upon. Attention is primarily paid to their specific behavioral, emotional, or educational "problems," and, thus, there is a strong inclination to divert attention both from the inadequacies of the educational institution itself [34] and what bureaucratic, social, and economic conditions caused the necessity of applying these constructs originally.

Let us now look a bit more deeply into the ethical configuration surrounding the idea of culpability. It is often the case that institutional labels, especially those that imply some sort of deviance—"slow learner," "discipline problem," "poor reader," may again serve as types found in educational settings—confer an inferior status on those so labeled. This is shot through with moral meanings and significance. Usually the "deviant" label has an *essentializing* quality in that a person's (here, a student's) entire relationship to an institution is conditioned by the category applied to this student. He or she *is* this and only this. The point is similar to Goffman's argument that the person to whom a deviant label is applied by others or by an institution is usually viewed as morally inferior, and his or her "condition" or behavior is quite often interpreted as evidence of *his or her* "moral culpability." [35] Thus, such labels are

[33] Robert A. Scott. "A Proposed Framework for Analyzing Deviance as a Property of Social Order." In: Scott and Douglas, *op. cit.,* p. 15. My stress.

[34] Bonnie Freeman. "Labeling Theory and Bureaucratic Structures in Schools." Unpublished paper, University of Wisconsin, Madison, 1973.

[35] Scott, *op. cit.,* p. 14. See also the discussion of deviance as a threat to taken-for-granted perspectives in Berger and Luckmann, *op. cit.* This is a complementary discussion to my own since once the hidden relationship between institutional constructs and the tacit maintenance of problematic practices in schools is illuminated, the commonsensical nature of these constructs becomes less accepted.

not neutral, at least not in their significance for the person. By the very fact that the labels are tinged with moral significance—not only is the child different but also inferior—their application has a profound impact. Labels once conferred are *lasting* due to the budgetary and bureaucratic reality of many schools (budgetary restrictions, lack of expertise in dealing with the "learning problems" of specific students). This fact makes it truly difficult to actually change the conditions which caused the child to be "a slow learner" or other category in the first place, which gives even more weight to the points I have been illuminating. Since only rarely is a student reclassified,[36] the effect of these labels is immense for they call forth forms of "treatment" which tend to confirm the person in the institutionally applied category.

It is often argued that such rhetorical devices as the labels to which I have been referring actually are used to help the child. After all, once so characterized the student can be given "proper treatment." However, just as plausible a case can be made that, given the reality of life in schools, the very definition of a student as someone in need of this particular treatment harms him or her.[37] As I have pointed out, such definitions are essentializing; they tend to be generalized to all situations which the individual confronts. As Goffman so potently illustrates, in total institutions—and schools share many of their characteristics—the label and all that goes with it is likely to be used by the individual's peers and custodians (for example, other children, teachers, and administrators) to *define* the individual. It governs nearly all of the conduct toward the person, and, more importantly, the definition ultimately governs the student's conduct toward these others, thereby acting to support a self-fulfilling prophecy.[38]

My point is not to deny that within the existing institutional framework of schooling there are such "things" as "slow learners," "underachievers," or "poorly motivated students" which we can commonsensically identify, though as I have contended such language hides the more basic issue of inquiring into the conditions

---

36 See: Aaron Cicourel and John Kitsuse. *The Educational Decision-Makers.* Indianapolis: Bobbs-Merrill Company, Inc., 1963. That this labeling process begins upon the student's initial entry into school, with the initial labels becoming increasingly crystallized, is documented in: Ray C. Rist. "Student Social Class and Teacher Expectation: The Self-Fulfilling Prophecy in Ghetto Education." *Harvard Educational Review,* 40: 411-51; August 1970.

37 Thomas S. Szasz. *Ideology and Insanity.* New York: Doubleday & Company, Inc., 1970. p. 149.

38 Erving Goffman. *Asylums.* New York: Doubleday & Company, Inc., 1961.

under which one group of people consistently labels others as deviant or applies some other taken-for-granted abstract category to them. Rather, I would like to argue that this linguistic system as it is commonly applied by school people does not serve a psychological or scientific function as much as they would like to suppose. To put it bluntly, it often serves to abase and degrade those individuals to whom the designations are so quickly given.[39]

A fact that should bring this argument into even clearer focus— that is, that the process of classification as it functions in educational research and practice is a moral and political act, not a neutral helping act—is the evidence that these labels are *massively* applied to the children of the poor and ethnic minorities much more so than the children of the more economically advantaged and politically powerful.

There is powerful recent empirical evidence to support parts of the arguments offered here. For example, Mercer's [40] analysis of the processes by which institutions like schools label individuals as, say, mentally retarded confirms this picture. Children with "nonmodal" sociocultural backgrounds and of minority groups predominate to a disproportionate degree in being so labeled. This is primarily due to diagnostic procedures in schools that were drawn almost totally from what she has called the dominance of "Anglocentrism" in schools, a form of ethnocentrism that causes school people to act as if their own group's life style, language, history, and value and normative structure were the "proper" guidelines against which all other people's activity should be measured. Not only were students from low socioeconomic and nonwhite backgrounds disproportionately labeled, but even more important, Mexican American and Black students, for instance, who were assigned the label of mental retardate were actually less "deviant" than whites. That is, they had *higher* IQ's than the "Anglos" who were so labeled.

Yet another fact should be noted. The school was most often the only institution to label these nonmodal students as retarded, primarily because of the prevailing assumptions of normality that were held by school personnel. These students performed quite well once outside the boundaries of that institution.

Mercer attributes this overdistribution of the mental retardate designation to the diagnostic, evaluative, and testing "machinery" of

[39] Szasz, *op. cit.*, p. 58.

[40] Jane R. Mercer. *Labeling the Mentally Retarded.* Berkeley, California: University of California Press, 1973.

the school.[41] Based as it is on statistical formulations that conform to problematic institutional assumptions concerning normality and deviance drawn from existing and often biased economic and political structures, it plays a large part in the process of channeling certain types of students into preexisting categories. The painful fact that this supposedly helpful machinery of diagnosis and remediation does not meet the reality of the child is given further documentation by Mehan's [42] important study of supposedly "normal" young children's reconstruction of the meaning of a testing situation and the evaluative instruments themselves. In essence, what he found was that, even in the most personally administered diagnostic testing, "testers" were apt to use speculative and inaccurate labels to summarize even more speculative and inaccurate results. The school tests actually *obscured* the children's real understanding of the materials and tasks, did not capture the children's varied abilities to reason adequately, and did not show "the negotiated, contextually bound measurement decisions that the tester makes while scoring children's behavior as 'correct' or 'incorrect.'" While this was especially true of "nonmodal" children (in this case, Spanish-speaking) it was also strikingly true for all other students as well.

If this research is correct, given the intense pressure for "accountability" today, the dominance of a process-product testing mentality, hence, will no doubt lead to even more problematic, anonymous, and socially and economically biased institutions due to the labels that stem from the testing process itself. The importance given to testing in schools cannot be underestimated in other ways. The labels that come from these "diagnoses" and assessments are not easily shaken off, and are in fact used by other institutions to continue the definitional ascription given by the school.

That is, it should be quite clear that not only does the school perform a central function of assigning labels to children in the process of sorting them and then distributing different knowledge, dispositions, and views of self to each of these labeled groups, but, just as important, the school occupies *the* central position in a larger

[41] *Ibid.*, pp. 96-123.

[42] Hugh Mehan. "Assessing Children's School Performance." In: Hans Peter Dreitzel, editor. *Childhood and Socialization.* New York: The Macmillan Company, 1973. pp. 240-64. For further discussion of how dominant modes of educational evaluation and assessment ignore the concrete reality of students and function in a conservative political and epistemological manner, see: Apple, "The Process and Ideology of Valuing in Educational Settings," *op. cit.*

network of other institutions. The labels imputed by the public schools are borrowed by legal, economic, health, and community institutions to define the individual in his or her contact with them as well.[43]

Thus, as institutions that are heavily influenced by statistical models of operation to define normality and deviance, models that are consistently biased toward extant social regularities, schools seem to have a disproportionate effect on labeling students. Because public schools depend almost exclusively on a statistical model for their normative frame, they generate categories of deviance that are filled with individuals largely from lower socioeconomic groups and ethnic minorities.[44] The ethical, political, and economic implications of this should be obvious.

This makes one notion very significant. The only serious way to make sense out of the imputation of labels in schools is to analyze the assumptions that underlie the definitions of competence these entail; and this can only be done in terms of an investigation of those who are in a position to *impose* these definitions.[45] Thus, the notion of *power* (what economic group or social class actually has it and how it is really being used) becomes critical if we are to understand why certain forms of social meanings—the authoritative election Blum talks of in the quote on the first page of this chapter—are used to select and organize the knowledge and perspectives educators employ to comprehend, order, and control activity in educational institutions.

One important latent function of schooling seems to be the distribution of forms of consciousness, often quite unequally, to students. Sociologically, then, through their appropriation of these dispositions and outlooks, students are able to be sorted into the various roles sedimented throughout the fabric of an advanced industrial society. The process of labeling occupies a subtle but essential place in this sorting. Because the designations, categories, and linguistic tools employed by educators, and especially by most members of the curriculum field of a behavioral persuasion, are perceived by them to have "scientific" status, there is little or no realization that the very language that they resort to is ideally suited

---

[43] Mercer, *op. cit.*, p. 96.

[44] *Ibid.*, pp. 60-61.

[45] Michael F. D. Young. "Curriculum and the Social Organization of Knowledge." In: Richard Brown, editor. *Knowledge, Education, and Cultural Change.* London: Tavistock, 1973. p. 350.

to maintain the bureaucratic rationality that has dominated schooling for so long a time.[46]

Edelman makes a similar point in discussing the way the distinctive language system of the "helping professions" is used to justify and marshal public support for professional practices that have profound political and ethical consequences.

Because the helping professions define other people's statuses (and their own), the special terms they employ to categorize clients and justify restrictions of their physical movements and of their moral and intellectual influence are especially revealing of the political functions language performs and of the multiple realities it helps create. Language is both a sensitive indicator and a powerful creator of background assumptions about people's levels of competence and merit. Just as any single numeral evokes the whole number scheme in our minds, so a term, a syntactic form, or a metaphor with political connotations can evoke and justify a power hierarchy in the person who used it and the groups that respond to it.[47]

Edelman's basic argument is not merely that the language forms educators and others use "arrange" their reality, but also that these forms covertly justify status, power, and authority. In short, one must examine the contradiction between a perspective that is there to help and at the same time actually serves the existing distribution of power in institutions and society.[48] This contradiction is difficult to miss in the language employed by school people.

Perhaps this argument is best summarized by quoting again from Edelman:

In the symbolic worlds evoked by the language of the helping professions, speculations and verified fact readily merge with each other. Language dispels the uncertainty in speculation, changes facts to make them serve status distinctions and reinforce ideology. The names for forms of mental illness, forms of delinquency, and for educational capacities are the basic terms. Each of them normally involves a high degree of unreliability in diagnosis, in prognosis, and in the prescription of rehabilitative treatments; but also entails unambiguous constraints upon clients, especially their confinement and subjection to the staff and the rules of a prison, school, or hospital. *The confinement and constraints*

[46] See: Freeman, *op. cit.*; and Herbert M. Kliebard. "Bureaucracy and Curriculum Theory." In: Vernon Haubrich, editor. *Freedom, Bureaucracy, and Schooling.* Washington, D.C.: Association for Supervision and Curriculum Development, 1971. pp. 74-93.

[47] Murray Edelman. "The Political Language of the Helping Professions." Unpublished paper, University of Wisconsin, Madison, 1973. pp. 3-4.

[48] *Ibid.*, p. 4.

are converted into liberating and altruistic acts by defining them as education, therapy, or rehabilitation. The arbitrariness and speculation in the diagnosis and the prognosis, on the other hand, are converted into clear and specific perceptions of the need for control [by the "helping group"]. Regardless of the arbitrariness or technical unreliability of professional terms, their political utility is manifest; they marshal popular support for professional discretion, concentrating public attention upon procedures and rationalizing in advance any failures of the procedures to achieve their formal objectives.[49]

That is, the supposedly neutral language of an institution, even though it rests upon highly speculative data and may be applied without actually being appropriate, provides a framework that legitimates control of major aspects of an individual's or a group's behavior. At the same time, by sounding scientific and "expert," it contributes to the quiescence of the public by focusing attention on its "sophistication" not on its political or ethical results. Thus, historically outmoded, and socially and politically conservative (and often educationally disastrous) practices are not only continued, but are made to sound as if they were actually more enlightened and ethically responsive ways of dealing with children.

As in other institutions where there is little choice about whether an individual (student, patient, inmate) may come or go as he or she pleases, by defining students through the use of such a quasi-scientific and quasi-clinical and therapeutic terminology and hence "showing" that students cannot be fully responsible for a large part of their activity within that institution (they are not adults; they have not reached a certain developmental stage; they have limited attention spans), educators need not face the often coercive aspects of their own activity.[50] Therefore, the ethical question of the nature of control in school settings does not have to be responded to. The clinical perspectives, the treatment language, the "helping" labels, all define it out of existence.

In what can almost act as a summary of this part of this essay, then, it is possible to argue that these criticisms are actually generic to clinical perspectives and helping labels [51] themselves as they func-

---

[49] *Ibid.*, pp. 7-8. My stress.

[50] Goffman, *op. cit.*, p. 115.

[51] Jane R. Mercer. "Labeling the Mentally Retarded." In: Earl Rubington and Martin S. Weinberg, editors. *Deviance: The Interactionist Perspective.* New York: The Macmillan Company, 1968. For a more complete treatment of the conservative posture of clinical and helping viewpoints, see: Apple, "The Process and Ideology of Valuing in Educational Settings," *op. cit.*

tion in education. The assumptions in which they are grounded are themselves open to question. These viewpoints are distinguished by a number of striking characteristics, each of which when combined with the others seems logically to lead to a conservative stance toward existing institutional arrangements. The first characteristic is that the researcher or practitioner studies or deals with those individuals who have already been labeled as different or deviant by the institution. In doing this, he or she adopts the values of the social system that defined the person as deviant. Furthermore, he or she assumes that the judgments made by the institution and based on these values are *the* valid measures of normality and competence without seriously questioning them.

Second, these clinical and helping perspectives have a strong tendency to perceive the difficulty as a problem with the individual, as something the individual rather than the institution lacks. Thus, combined with the assumption that the official definition is the only right definition, almost all action is focused on changing the individual rather than the defining agent, the larger institutional context. Third, researchers and practitioners who accept the institutional designations and definitions tend to assume that all of the people within these categories are the same. There is an assumption of homogeneity. In this way, individual complexity is automatically flattened.

Also, it can well be argued that there are strong motivations for use already built into these labels and the processes and expertise behind them. That is, the "professional helpers" who employ the supposedly diagnostic and therapeutic terminologies *must* find (and hence create) individuals who fit the categories, otherwise the expertise is useless. This is probably a general educational fact. Once a "new" (but always limited) tool or perspective for "helping" children is generated, it tends to expand beyond the "problem" for which it was initially developed. The tools (here diagnostic, therapeutic, and linguistic) also have the effect of redefining past issues in these other areas into problems the tool is capable of dealing with.[52] The best example is behavior modification. While applicable to a limited range of difficulties in schools, it becomes both a

[52] An interesting point should be made here. Persons employing clinical perspectives in dealing with health or deviance are apt to label people as "sick" rather than "well" in most instances to avoid the danger of what might happen to the "patient" if they are wrong. Here, one more motivation for "finding" individuals to fit institutional categories can be uncovered. See: Thomas Scheff. *Being Mentally Ill: A Sociological Theory.* Chicago: Aldine Publishing Company, 1966. pp. 105-106.

diagnostic language and a form of "treatment" for a wider range of "student problems." Thus, for instance, its increasing use and acceptance in ghetto schools and elsewhere with "disruptive" children, or with entire classes as is becoming more the case, really acts as a cloak to cover the political fact that the nature of the existing educational institutions is unresponsive to a large portion of students. In addition, its treatment language acts to hide the alienating wage-product relationship that has been established and called education. Finally, the perspective, by defining itself clinically, covers the very real moral questions that must be raised concerning the appropriateness of the technique itself in dealing with students who have no choice about being in the institution.

Labeling: Part of a Complex Avoidance Process

One of the points that complements the foregoing discussion is that those people who are perceived as being different or deviant from normal institutional expectations are threatening to the day to day life of schools, to the normal pattern of operation that is constant and so often relatively sterile. In this regard, the labeling act can be seen as part of a complex avoidance process. It acts to preserve the tenuous nature of many interpersonal relationships within schools. But even more important, it enables people like teachers, administrators, curriculum workers, and other school people to confront stereotypes rather than individuals since schools cannot deal with distinctive characteristics of individuals to any significant degree. There is a good deal of research that supports the fact that differences from institutional expectations often result in avoidance reactions on the part of people who confront these individuals who are "deviant." [53] Thus, stereotyping and labeling are heightened and the comforting illusion that children are being helped is preserved.

Based on the preceding analysis, one other crucial point should be noted at this time. Of particular import for curricular and other educational research, then, is to argue *against* the temptation to use

[53] Schur, *op. cit.*, p. 51. This is not to say that all labeling can be done away with. It is to say, however, that we must begin to raise serious critical questions on how specific labels and the massiveness of the reality these categories represent function in school settings. On the fact that stereotypes or typifications are necessary for perception (but are also linked to ideological presuppositions) see: Peter L. Berger and Thomas Luckmann. *The Social Construction of Reality.* New York: Doubleday & Company, 1966.

officially collected statistics based on these officially defined categories that are often readily available. Rather, the more critical
question to ask is "What assumptions underpin the constructs within
which these data were generated?" [54] By raising questions of this
type one may illuminate the very potent normative implications
involved when educators designate students by some specific institutional abstraction. The distribution of labels among a student population is actually a process by which one social group makes value
judgments about the appropriateness or inappropriateness of another
group's action. If such a perspective is correct, then the points I
have been articulating suggest that a good deal of investigation
remains to be done showing how the meaning structures of dominant
groups in American society when imposed upon schools have rather
wide ethical, political, and social implications in that they may
assist in sorting out individuals according to class, race, and sex
quite early in life.

These are quite frankly difficult questions. Yet, in the very act
of searching for relief from the all too real moral responsibilities
and dilemmas of caring for (here meant in an almost religious sense)
and influencing others, educators have done what Szasz calls "mys-
tifying and technicizing their problems of living." What this has to
say about the dominance in educational thought of psychological
models and metaphors based upon a "strict science" image [55] is
quite significant.

The orientations which so predominate curriculum theory, and
indeed have consistently dominated it in the past, effectively obscure
and often deny the profound ethical issues educators face. They
transform these dilemmas into engineering problems or puzzles that
are amenable to technical "professional" solutions. Perhaps the best
example is the field's nearly total reliance on perspectives drawn
from the psychology of learning. The terminology drawn from this
psychology and its allied fields is quite inadequate since it neglects

[54] *Ibid.*

[55] The term "strict science" refers here to fields whose fundamental
interests reflect and are dialectically related to the dominant interests of
advanced industrial economic systems and thus are grounded in process-
product or purposive-rational logic. These interests are in technical rules,
control, and certainty. Among the fields one could point to are behavioral
psychology and sociology. See: Jürgen Habermas. "Knowledge and Interest."
In: Dorothy Emmet and Alasdair MacIntyre, editors. *Sociological Theory and
Philosophical Analysis.* New York: The Macmillan Company, 1970. pp. 36-54;
and Michael W. Apple. "Scientific Interests and the Nature of Educational
Institutions." In: William Pinar, editor. *Curriculum Theorizing: The Recon-
ceptualists.* Berkeley, California: McCutchan Publishing Corporation, 1974.

or at best tends to draw attention from the basically political and moral character of social existence and human development.

The language of reinforcement, learning, negative feedback, and so forth is a rather weak tool for dealing with the continual encroachment of chaos upon order, with the creation and recreation of personal meaning and interpersonal institutions, with the political nature of schooling and other institutions, and with notions such as responsibility and justice in conduct with others. In essence, the language of psychology as it is exercised in curriculum "de-ethicizes and depoliticizes human relations and personal conduct." [56]

For example, much of our busy endeavor to define operational objectives and to state student "outcomes" in behavioral terms may be interpreted as exactly that—busywork, if I may use commonsense terminology for the moment. That is, because of the field's preoccupation with the wording of its goal statements and "output measures," attention is diverted from the crucial political and moral implications of our activity as educators. In this way means are turned into ends and children are transformed into manipulable and anonymous abstractions called "learners." Speaking of the field of sociology, though quite the same things could be said about a large portion of curricular language and research, Friedrichs articulates part of the problem clearly.

What sociologists appear completely unaware of is the long-run impact of coming to *conceive* of one's fellows as manipulable. Language— and the choice among symbols it entails—pervades all meaningful social action, either overtly or covertly, consciously or unconsciously. The symbolic manipulation of man cannot be wholly isolated from the rest of a person's symbolically mediated relationships with others. As man's intellectual life more and more demands such symbolic manipulation, he runs the increasing risk of conceiving man in other areas of his life in terms that invite or are particularly amenable to a means-ends relationship rather than those that support an attitude toward others as ends in themselves.[57]

Thus, the manipulative ethos of a larger society is found within curriculum discourse in the basic behavioral and treatment language and categories used for even conceiving of educational relationships. It thereby creates and reinforces patterns of interaction that not only

[56] Szasz, *op. cit.*, p. 2.

[57] Robert W. Friedrichs. *A Sociology of Sociology*. New York: The Free Press, 1970. pp. 172-73.

reflect but actually embody the interests in certainty and control that dominate the consciousness of advanced industrial societies.

Furthermore, it should be clear that no single attribute of an individual can be employed to define that person.[58] Nor is it the case that any one model or language system can exhaust the complexity of an individual's response to his or her situation. The propensity of curriculum specialists and other educators to define the student as "learner" and thus to design an environment which corresponds to this one attribute of being human is but one example of this sort of category error in educational thought.

As a final part of this section, let me attempt through alternative examples to show that these conceptions, categories, and labels are, in fact, commonsensical and ideological not preordained or "natural." In our society, a high premium is put on intelligence. Schools are obviously organized around and value such a concept. The fact that they limit it to quite constricted and mostly verbal versions of it is important but not the point here. Rather, we should note that it is possible to describe other conceptions around which our educational and social institutions could be organized and our technology designed. For instance, envision a society in which physical *grace* not our overly constricted definitions of competence and intelligence was the most valued characteristic.[59] Those who were clumsy or merely reached lower categories of grace might then be discriminated against. The culture's educational structure would categorize individuals according to their "capacity for grace." The technology would be so designed that it would require elegance in motion for it to be employed.

Besides physical grace (which is really not too outlandish a concept) one could also point to the possibility of valuing, say, moral excellence. After all, this type of dispositional element is one of the things that education is all about, isn't it? However, as the literature on the hidden curriculum strongly suggests, the basic regularities of schools excel in teaching the opposite. For example, because of the dominance of evaluation—both public and private, of oneself and one's peers—in school settings, subterfuge, hiding one's real feelings, joy at someone else's failure, and so forth, are quite effectively taught. This occurs merely by the student's living

[58] Ollman, *op. cit.*, p. 111. For a less Marxist, but no less critical, phenomenological approach to this position see: Abraham Heschel. *Who Is Man?* Palo Alto, California: Stanford University Press, 1965.

[59] Lewis A. Dexter. "On the Politics and Sociology of Stupidity in Our Society." In: Howard S. Becker, editor. *The Other Side.* New York: The Free Press, 1964. pp. 37-49.

within an institution and having to cope with its density, power, and competitiveness.[60]

The implications of these counterexamples are rather significant for they indicate that a serious attempt at changing the accepted commonsense conceptions of competence *in practice* may need to change the basic regularities of the institutional structure of schooling itself. The regularities themselves are the "teaching devices" that communicate lasting norms and dispositions to students, that instruct children in "how the world really is." It is important to notice the critical implications of each of these alternative conceptions for the business, advertising, and other institutions of the larger society as well. They act as potent reminders that criticism of many of the characteristics of schools and social, political, and cultural criticism must go hand in hand. Schools do not exist in a vacuum.

For instance, much of the labeling process that I have been examining here has at its roots a concern for efficiency. That is, schools as agents of social control in some sense need to operate as efficient organizations and labeling helps a good deal in this.[61] As much activity as possible must be rationalized and made goal specific so that cost effectiveness and smoothness of operation are heightened and "waste," inefficiency, and uncertainty are eliminated. Furthermore, conflict and argumentation over goals and procedures must be minimized so as not to jeopardize existing goals and procedures. After all, there is a good deal of economic and psychological investment in these basic institutional regularities. Techniques for the control and manipulation of difference must be developed, then, in order to prevent disorder of any significant sort from encroaching on institutional life. If significant difference (either intellectual, aesthetic, valuative, or normative) is found, it must be redefined into categories that can be handled by existing bureaucratic assumptions. The fact that these assumptions are relatively unexamined and are, in fact, *self-confirming* as long as educators employ categories that grow out of them is forgotten.

However, to point to the schools as the originators of this concern for efficiency above all else in education is too limited an appraisal. The roots of this technocratic perspective lie in a taken-

[60] See: Jules Henry. *Culture Against Man.* New York: Random House, 1963; and Philip Jackson. *Life in Classrooms.* New York: Holt, Rinehart, and Winston, 1968. Goffman's notion of "secondary adjustments" is quite helpful in interpreting parts of the hidden curriculum. Goffman, *op. cit.*, p. 189.

[61] Schur, *op. cit.*, p. 96.

for-granted ideology that provides the constitutive framework for thought and action in all advanced industrial societies, an instrumental ideology that places efficiency, standardized technique, growth, and consensus at its very heart. Consequently, the caughtness of schools and especially the curriculum field in what Kliebard has called a factory model [62] is part of a larger social problem concerning the lack of responsiveness of our major institutions to human needs and sentiment. To lose sight of this is to miss much of the real problem. There are questions, though, that can be asked within an educational framework that could challenge portions of this ideology. A few of these questions will be pointed to in the final part of this analysis.

Toward Asking Some Salient Questions

This essay has sought to raise a number of questions regarding some of the taken-for-granted underpinnings shared by groups of school people. It would not be complete without at least pointing out a direction that curriculum scholarship and practice could take if the field is to be reconstructed. While the specific path suggested here is tentative, the author has few doubts that the general direction is appropriate.

Our movement should be progressively away from the current "quasi-scientific" and engineering framework that now guides most of the field's endeavors and should consistently move toward a political and ethical structure. While there is certainly a need for technical expertise in the field—after all, curriculum specialists are called upon to assist in the designing and creating of concrete environments based on our differing educational visions—all too often a technical and efficiency perspective supplies the problems, and other considerations such as those analyzed in this chapter are afterthoughts, if they are indeed considered at all. A more appropriate relationship might require that educational engineering and technical competence be secured firmly within a framework that continually seeks to be self-critical and places one person's responsibility to treat another person ethically and justly at the center of its deliberations. [63]

[62] Kliebard, *op. cit.*

[63] This is obviously a difficult analytic issue as well as a moral concern. A good place to begin would be the impressive work of Rawls. See especially: John Rawls. *A Theory of Justice.* Cambridge, Massachusetts: Harvard University Press, 1971.

Habermas extends these arguments and their implications for the reconstruction of curriculum research and practice. He holds that the controlling and bureaucratized institutions of advanced industrial society require increasing scientific and technical knowledge. The research communities, for example, generate new rationalities and techniques that make further control and domination of individuals and groups by an instrumental and technical ideology possible. However, while these communities produce data that support existing institutionalized rubrics and mechanisms for control, they are also in an increasingly pivotal strategic position. Because the basic social norms that ideally guide the various "scientific" communities rest strongly upon a foundation of open and honest communication,[64] there is a potential within these groups for the recognition of the unnecessary control and domination that exist in many of the institutions of society. In addition, the turning around of even a small portion of the community of educational scholars and practitioners to recognize the quasi-neutral perspectives that dominate their rationality, language, and investigations would have the positive effect of illuminating the way educational and other forms of social research miss the ethical and political meaning of their work.[65] In other words, the development of a critical perspective within the educational community can "contribute to the creation of alternative programs of research and development" that challenge the commonsense assumptions that underpin the field.

Just as important, in this way . . .

Knowledge can be generated that relates to the needs of the peoples who are trying to build social community, resist cultural manipulation, facilitate decentralization movements, and in general contribute to the actualization of human needs that are otherwise ignored. By reorienting the scientific community, or at least a significant section of it, critical theory can become a material force for change by counteracting the current drift of science toward the formation and implementation of state policy.[66]

It should be clear, therefore, that these arguments imply [67] that

[64] See: Norman Storer. *The Social System of Science.* New York: Holt, Rinehart, and Winston, 1966.

[65] Schroyer, *The Critique of Domination, op. cit.*, pp. 165-66.

[66] *Ibid.*, p. 172.

[67] See, for example: Michael W. Apple and Thomas Brady. "Toward Increasing the Potency of Student Rights Claims." In: Vernon F. Haubrich and Michael W. Apple, editors. *Schooling and the Rights of Children.* Berkeley, California: McCutchan Publishing Corporation, 1975.

advocacy models of research and practice are critically needed if substantial progress is to be made.

Reality, however, has to be faced here. To most people, the very idea of regaining any real control over social institutions and personal development is abstract and "nonsensical." In general, people see society's economic, social, and educational institutions as basically self-directing, with little need for their participation and with little necessity for them to communicate and argue over the ends and means of these same institutions. Even though the disintegration of aspects of family life, schools, or work, is often evident, the basic categories of industrialized logic have become so commonsensical that people no longer even see a need for emancipation, other than an anomic sense that pervades certain segments of the population. This makes the development of a *critical* curriculum community, for example, all the more essential since it is here that a part of the systematic criticism of the basic categories that grow out of and help produce problematic institutions can originate. That is, one of the fundamental conditions of emancipation is the ability to "see" the actual functionings of institutions in all their positive *and* negative complexity, to illuminate the contradictions of extant regularities,[68] and, finally, to assist others in "remembering" the possibilities of spontaneity and choice.

This means that curriculum specialists must take an advocacy position on a number of critical fronts. Among the most important would be that of student rights. Since curriculum as a field has as one of its primary concerns the task of creating access to knowledge and tradition in a variety of forms, the question of a student's right to have free access to information and to public expression based on this *cannot* be divorced from our own pursuit of just educative environments.

Not only should an advocacy and critical model guide us in students' rights questions, but other issues abound in the increasing use of therapeutic models in education, models that serve as excuses to change the individual child rather than the social and intellectual structure of the school to make it more responsive and responsible.

Consider, for instance, the current rapid growth of a "treatment" language on the part of educators. Behavior modification or a behavioral objectives approach again can offer good examples of this. Educators talk of giving certain specifiable "treatments" to bring about certain specifiable "results" or outcomes. Discounting the fact that the supposed cause and effect relationships between

[68] Schroyer, *The Critique of Domination, op. cit.*, p. 248.

treatment and outcome are rather psychologically and logically difficult to establish, there are ethical and especially legal implications concerning the perspectives out of which clinical and therapeutic categories, labels, and procedures arise that must be brought to the fore.

Many legal scholars have taken the position that before therapeutic programs of any sort may be engaged in, there are several criteria that must be satisfied. First, we must be satisfied that the motive behind the therapeutic program is truly therapeutic and *that it is unlikely to be perverted into merely a mechanism of social control.* All too much of curriculum work in the past, however, has functioned in exactly this way. This is especially true of the control ideology in the evaluation and testing movement, though much the same thing could be said about many educational practices we continue to employ, the types of institutions we design, and the forms of interaction that dominate them.[69] This questioning must be seen not only in relation to the past and present but also in terms of future uses. No broad programs of diagnosis and treatment, of remediation, amelioration, and "help," should be given institutional endorsement on the grounds that practitioners require a good deal more flexibility in the methods they may use to be more effective, without at the same time showing clearly that the procedure does not exceed what is necessary to reach its goals (if in fact the goals and means are ethically, politically, and educationally *just*).[70]

Second, the program must demonstrate, *prior to its implementation*, that it is capable of accomplishing its goals. Without this, "the program may become an intervention into people's lives and liberties for no acceptable purpose. The individual will have been sacrificed, and society will have gained nothing." Third, and perhaps most important for my own analysis here, *any undesirable side effects, any latent outcomes of such interference into the life of an individual that can possibly be foreseen must be known beforehand and properly weighed.*[71] As I have shown here, some of the contradictions

---

[69] Clarence Karier. "Ideology and Evaluation." In: Michael W. Apple, Michael J. Subkoviak, and Henry S. Lufler, Jr., editors. *Educational Evaluation: Analysis and Responsibility.* Berkeley, California: McCutchan Publishing Corporation, 1974; and Karier, Violas, and Spring, *op. cit.*

[70] The argumentation over whether these means and ends *are* just is not easy and cannot be reduced to technical procedures such as pools of goals or "needs assessment" where power and rationality still reside only at the top. On the concept of justice, see John Rawls, *op. cit.*

[71] Nicholas N. Kittrie. *The Right To Be Different: Deviance and Enforced Therapy.* Baltimore: Johns Hopkins Press, 1971. p. 336.

and latent ethical and political outcomes of the labeling process and all that goes with it are indeed profound.

Educators have much to learn from the fact that new and increasingly subtle techniques of behavior control seem to generate an impetus that causes them to be generalized beyond their immediate situation. Therefore, any proposed use of them must be examined quite carefully and at least must embody procedural safeguards for students and parents that prevent the abuse of the programs and which guarantee that they are compatible with a pluralistic and diverse society.[72]

These legal cautions and safeguards are but one step, however, and in fact represent a limited approach to the problem of control and the ethical uses of our commonsense language and perspectives. A second step is to critically examine and raise serious questions about the very basis of these programs and processes that have their foundation in commonsense assumptions. As one final everyday example, it is possible to see the growth of, say, a therapy model in such things as the value clarification materials and techniques found in social studies.[73] Do these things merely signify amateur therapy (after all, education is *not* therapy), examples of the power of schooling in extending its rationalizing ethos to even the most private and personal dispositions of students so that they can be better controlled? Are such approaches indicative of the need on the part of a society dominated by interests in control, instrumental rationality, and certainty to "produce" individuals who feel at home in institutions that have little personal meaning? While these questions are not easily answered or even easily stated in a way that makes them potent, they must be examined if curriculum specialists and other educators are to be aware of the latent ideological functions of their work.

It should be clear, therefore, that part of the task of establishing a firmer basis for the curriculum field is for its practitioners to distance themselves from those who control economic and political power and the now rather limited routes to them in this society. By this I do not mean that curriculum specialists should not engage in political and economic argumentation and analysis. *Quite the contrary is the case.* Rather the members of the field need to stand

---

[72] *Ibid.*, p. 339.

[73] See the excellent analysis of value clarification that documents the fact that it basically *is* a form of therapy by: Alan L. Lockwood. "A Critical View of Values Clarification." Madison: University of Wisconsin, 1974. (Mimeographed.)

back from their position of totally accepting the institutions and the rationality that prevail in advanced industrial societies like our own. Obviously, this involves a rather difficult form of questioning. However, unless we look to other perspectives such as the critical scholarship to which I have referred, ones which may enable us to raise more important issues, we are being less than honest to ourselves. As I have tried to convey, much of the commonsense activity in which we engage is not neutral nor is it often helpful to the concrete persons who inhabit the existing role of student in schools.

This process of stepping back also requires some very exacting analytic scholarship as well. We must examine in depth our over-dependence on "scientific" models of procedure, especially those drawn from fields whose constitutive interests embody strict control and certainty when dealing with the problem of human action.[74] The important questions to ask here are:

1. What *should* be the relationship between curriculum thought and other disciplines upon which it may draw for support, insight, and guidance? [75]

2. In what ways can the field of curriculum employ insights taken from disciplines with an interest in technical control and certainty and still maintain an emancipatory interest itself? [76]

3. What other forms of "rationality" can be used to illuminate the complexity of the human situation curriculum specialists confront?

4. If it is indeed important to employ a number of other perspectives that enable critical reflection, besides the quasi-scientific approaches that have governed the field in the past, how are we to prevent just as potent a difficulty that lies at the heart of many of the problems of current and past curriculum scholarship—that is,

[74] For an analysis of these constitutive interests and alternatives to them, see: Apple, "Scientific Interests and the Nature of Educational Institutions," *op. cit.*

[75] See: Joseph Schwab. *The Practical: A Language for Curriculum.* Washington, D.C.: National Education Association, 1970, for one position on this issue. While Schwab's essay is provocative, it is also often circular in its arguments. However, very few others have dealt with the question in any significant fashion.

[76] One possible answer to this problem can be found in: Dwayne Huebner. "Implications of Psychological Thought for the Curriculum." In: Glenys G. Unruh and Robert R. Leeper, editors. *Influences in Curriculum Change.* Washington, D.C.: Association for Supervision and Curriculum Development, 1968. pp. 28-37.

the borrowing of very surface concepts and constructs from these lending fields, constructs that become quickly outmoded and are inaccurate representations of the complexity of the original? [77]

One final set of questions, I believe, needs to be faced quite openly. Can we as educators honestly cope with the probability that certainty will not be forthcoming, that all our answers will be situational and filled with ambiguity? With this in mind, how do we commit ourselves to action? Part of the response to this is the realization that our very commitment to rationality in the widest sense of the term *requires* us to begin the dialectic of critical understanding that will be part of political praxis. Yet another part of the response is illuminated by my arguments in this essay. Even our "neutral" activity may not be so. One has no choice but to be committed.

[77] See: Apple, "The Adequacy of Systems Management Procedures in Education," *op. cit.*

THE STORY OF THE AMERICAN NEGRO

Section III
COMMITMENT

Toward an Agenda for Action

THE PREVIOUS SECTIONS OF THIS YEARBOOK have attempted to provide a context for criticism and a set of critiques with differing orientations within the general framework of an analysis of "in whose interest" and "who makes" educational decisions.

Essentially, all of the critiques accept the position that schools are intricately connected with the broader social system and both reflect and perpetuate socially dominant interests. There is, in effect, a consensus among us that social institutions are indeed only superficially separate and that cultural, political, and socioeconomic forces are functionally interwoven throughout the texture of all of them; that the dominant interests in society are the basic controllers of the decisions made within institutional settings; and . . . that the decisions made *are* in the "best" interests of the dominant group(s).

Further, we all agree that the data available from a variety of sources clearly show that the democratic values which we hold are not functioning socially, economically, politically, or culturally in egalitarian terms for different sexes, different races, different ethnic minorities, different social classes, and different age groups. Thus, for example, we reject the hypothesis that the unequal status of women, blacks, Latinos, adolescents, retired persons, and wage/salary earners in comparison to the wealthy in society is simply a historical coincidence that has accumulated over the centuries by random social forces. On the contrary we believe that inequity, inequality, injustice, unequal access, and preferential treatment are built into a total systemic pattern; and that these circumstances serve

151

the interests of those groups and persons in our social world who have the power to make decisions that affect the lives of everyone.

At the heart of the matter, persons concerned about schooling must decide whether schooling is basically a process of training or a process of educating. If it is to be a training operation then there is little need to be concerned about anything but teaching basic skills, information, and developing adequate role players for the present socioeconomic system. But if we choose to try to educate, then it becomes quite a different matter.

Perhaps the question today is "Dare the schools attempt to educate?" For as Nietzsche remarked (in "Schopenhauer as Educator"), "your educators can be nothing more than your liberators." "Education is liberation, a rooting out of all the weeds, rubbish, and vermin from around the buds of the plant."

Liberation must mean both freedom from unreasonable restraint (domination by others' interests), and freedom to develop potential (participation in decision making). Thus, the point being made throughout the Yearbook has been that liberation is not simply liberation from the personal domination of one person over another, but liberation in a deeper sense of changing the basic socioeconomic and cultural conditions that structure the dominating personal behaviors in our society. As such, liberation is a morally directed political activity.

The fundamental question becomes "What must progressive educators do?" and the question of action is a historical question rather than simply a moral response to present conditions. Action is based upon an analysis of historical and contemporary forces and conditions rather than simply on moral precepts or sentiment. This point of view stands in direct contrast to the liberal view that action is based on the desire to take a "righteous stand" or "bear moral witness," and then to compromise. This stand reflected in reformist action is easily tolerated within the existing political reality. "Taking a moral stand" can be an important step in the development of political consciousness, but educators who are serious about progressive movement must see it *as a step on the way* to mature political action based upon deeper historical and contemporary analysis.

It should be clear that educators are not simply members of a community of other school people. More important is the fact that they are members of a larger collectivity whose values provide the fundamental framework for their thought and action. This fact cuts two ways. First, it means that any critical act in an educational sense is by necessity an act that is critical of the dominant normative structure of the larger society. Educational criticism, hence, becomes cultural, political, and economic criticism as well. Without the latter, the former is impotent. Second, the setting of educators within a more basic social group means that extensive investigations are required to demonstrate to other educators and a concerned citizenry that concrete linkages exist between personal, social, and economic injustice and education's models of inquiry, of talking about schooling, of "helping" children, and so forth. That is, the sense that education is always moral and political activity in some degree must be the constitutive framework from which any committed educator can act.

A Perspective That Gives Meaning

All of us are committed to a variety of ways of altering the conditions that cause these problems to evolve, and all of us sense certain paths that can be taken and can be suggested to others that will be at least a beginning in changing these conditions.

For a number of reasons, however, it would be impossible to spell out a list of definitive actions that all committed educators should engage in, even if we can specify general organizational needs. First, situations differ. Some types of activity are appropriate for certain specific points in time, in certain specific institutional contexts, while others would be less than helpful. Second, and just as important, random and uncoordinated action may ultimately hurt rather than help. Working to change the modes of domination in schooling and other institutional settings requires a vision of justice and fairness behind it, a perspective that gives meaning to concrete actions and shows why they should be engaged in.

To borrow slightly from Silberman, though in another more political context to be sure, we need "minded" political and educational action. For some of us, that "mindedness" will come from a vision of radically different social and economic relations than now exist, for others it will have its roots in a more immediate concern for eliminating the class bias, racism, and sexism that often lie at the heart of many institutions in our society. These positions will be deeply felt and may in fact lead to significant conflict among groups of people who are concerned about the lack of responsiveness in our dominant institutions. What is important, however, is that these groups establish linkages to one another, that they begin to work cooperatively on a number of fronts—economic, cultural, political, legal, and educational—to provide the first openings in a struggle to make our institutions responsive to the people they serve.

Myths and realities of schooling in our time can only be transformed through understanding the present power structure in and outside education and taking cooperative action toward redistributing that power. What are the critical action points for disclosing and dealing with these realities? Digging through the levels and varied dimensions of reality and myths surrounding schooling requires informed, determined, and cooperative group action. Starting with your own situation, whether student, teacher, parent, staff, administrator, the questions (again) that must be asked are first "Whose interests are being served in the present order of things?" and, second, "Who is making the decisions?" Both questions deal with the distribution of power: Who dominates; Who are the dominated?

Furthermore, there are certain actions that are necessary to maintain political and democratic rights in schools. While certain portions of this volume have focused on student rights, given the growth of repressive measures taken against activist teachers (perhaps because of the ease with which a replacement can be hired) the guaranteeing of political and democratic rights of teachers as well as students is also of considerable importance.

Teachers are low-paid and exploited professionals, paid by the state to carry out its program for socializing and training the work force. A large majority of the teachers are women, not because women are intrinsically better suited to teaching, but because they can be hired more cheaply than men. This is so because in our economic system women are a reserve labor force compelled to work for substandard wages when they work outside the home. The use of women in the teaching profession enables the state to carry out its "educational" program at the lowest cost. This low-cost plan is supplemented by the ideology which says that for most women wages are merely a "supplemental" income (the husband providing the "real" income regardless of the type of work he does or the amount he earns) and that therefore they should be willing to work for less. In addition, the ideology is promoted in teacher-training programs that education is a "service to the nation" and that, therefore, teachers should be people who are willing to accept the intrinsic rewards of "service" in place of more just wages.

Promotion, which, in the education profession, means essentially entry into the administrative hierarchy, goes in overwhelming disproposition to men. In effect, this amounts to buying off that sector of the teaching profession that the male supremacist ideology of the profession posits has the "greatest need" for higher wages (because men earn the "real" rather than merely "supplemental" income). The effect of this economic co-opting is (a) to remove from the teaching force those most likely to be militant in the demand for higher wages and (b) to ensure ideological conformity to the State's educational program among those who enter the administration. Conformity among the teachers themselves is assured by placing decisions of hiring, firing, and tenure in the hands of those who have accepted an economic advantage along with its ideological content (including male supremacy) and have thereby moved out of the ranks of teachers to become principals or higher-level administrators.

In spite of these facts, many rank and file teachers over the years have shown great militancy in the struggle for better wages and working conditions, and for basic democratic rights in the conduct of their professional work. The evolution of this militancy has been similar to that of other working sectors: the formation of unions that started out representing the interest of teachers but that have gradually become centralized into a national bureaucratic organization or absorbed into the AFL-CIO labor aristocracy, which functions primarily in the interest of the aristocracy itself. Thus teachers, many of whom have fought hard for the rights of union representation, are left without any organization that will lead their fight for decent wages and living conditions, or that will help them protect what very little freedom they have in making basic decisions about the content and methodology of their educational work.

The manipulation of large amounts of federal money, coupled with collaboration among publishers, university professors, and state school boards and administrators has resulted in movement toward even greater uniformity in the actual content and methodology of education despite the glossy illusion of "pluralism" in both areas.

The result of the previously mentioned conditions is that teachers have been unable to secure an adequate cost of living increase in their already inadequate wages; or to protect, let alone extend, their democratic rights with regard to the conditions, conduct, and content of their work.

When placed in the context of the general political situation, the teacher can be seen to face very hard years. As the contradiction between labor and capital intensifies, teachers, along with other workers, will find their living standards increasingly under attack. Ideological uniformity, as well as male chauvinism and white supremacy as particular forms of this ideology, will be further extended.

Democratic rights including the right to conduct one's professional activities in a manner consistent with the interest of the liberation of dominated and exploited people, will be further curtailed. Teachers must understand that the attacks they face are also being faced now and in the immediate future by an increasingly large sector of the entire wage earning and salaried populace; that is, by all but the most affluent sectors of the country.

From this analysis two tactical principles follow. First, teachers must draw the lines sharply between those who will fight for decent wages and the right to teach in a manner that truly serves the liberation of people and those who would prefer to perpetuate the domination of special interests by endlessly compromising and acquiescing to the political system. Second, teachers must overcome the elitist ideology that gives them the pretence of belonging to a profession that is "higher" than the working class, recognizing fully that in carrying out the work of the State, they are a specially exploited sector of workers; and on this basis they must form strong alliances with other organizations of dominated people who face the same attacks they do.

The oppressive domination of our young people in schools is a favorite topic of liberal school criticism. While we agree that there is severe oppression in schools, we do not agree with liberal criticism that traces the oppression to breakdowns, inadequacies, or flaws in our state system of education that can be corrected through minor reforms, nor do we agree with the so-called "radical" critics who would "abolish" the schools altogether, thereby putting the young even more directly at the mercy of a highly dominated and controlled economy. Nor do we agree that "alternative" schools, either inside or outside of the public school system, can offer anything of importance to the great masses of children now in public schools. We see the oppression of youth as a direct expression of special socioeconomic interests' domination of social relations. Consequently, any action aimed at ending the oppression of youth must be understood and developed as a part of changing this economic domination. Since students, both in their situation as students and as a reserve and future labor force, face the same economic and political attacks that teachers and other workers face, political action around the professional work of educators should focus on three demands: (a) democracy for teachers and students in the schools; (b) a curriculum that reveals to students the nature of dominant socioeconomic structures in place of one that indoctrinates them to be passive servants; and (c) the right to link the education and the political struggle of students with the education and the political struggle of all dominated persons.

We do not suggest that "irrational activism" is any more desirable than "neutral intellectualizing." The key to progressive action lies in acting in terms of a conception of the historical and contemporary nature of the system, and constant reflection on the consequences and adequacy of our actions in terms of the conception we hold.

Thus, it seems to us that some of the educators' concerns must be conceptual (in the best sense of the term), some must be political, and others must be practical. However, these are by no means disparate or separate, indeed they cannot really be divorced from one another in action.

Arenas for Action

To illustrate a conception of praxis as action and reflection, involving conceptual, political, and practical activity, the following general ideas discovered through work in varying educational contexts are presented. They are presented as four basic action arenas which must be considered and constantly dealt with in praxis. They represent, in a sense, change variables and also bases for strategies of action.

1. *Ideology*—Progressive change (of any kind) necessitates a shared framework for structural, social, and educational analysis and a common set of shared values, which may be called an ideology. The important point here is that there be a shared language which describes reality and that a common set of ethical and/or moral judgments of the reality be shared. Further, this shared analysis suggests some direction toward which we wish to move.

We have suggested throughout that a class analysis of school and society based on the fundamental values of Judeo-Christian culture provide a framework for a powerful shared conception that is consistent with the contradictions we see in today's world. We have among ourselves a broad interpretation of class analysis, varying from a general concern for domination to a highly specific Marxist analysis. In any case, it is clear to us that we must look beyond the individual to groups of people sharing similar circumstances in the socioeconomic structure.

2. *Developing Support Systems*—A further necessary step is the identification of allies and expertise, sharing the general ideology,

who can be called upon to provide both broader social legitimization and technical advice and to help in the development of action goals. University personnel, members of the legal profession, and other lay people and groups may be important sources of support.

3. *Developing Affiliative Groups*—Regardless of support it is necessary to have groups of persons sharing similar ideas and goals meeting together frequently to exchange ideas, reinforce each other's commitments, and see their ideas and goals in a broader perspective than one school or one system. Further, affiliative groups are growth stimulating through the development of personal relationships and by the continual raising of consciousness that takes place through dialog.

4. *Developing a Common Pool of Resources and Techniques.* Goals and ideals are meaningful only in praxis, through action and reflection. Thus, how to realize goals and with the help of what resources become a constant and critical set of problems. Thus, focusing upon and creating techniques, roles, resources, and facilities for developing changes are a major agenda item for affiliative groups, and a major contribution of support groups.

A Possible Agenda

There are a variety of action agendas that could be developed from the ideas expressed in this Yearbook. Yet it seems clear that the direction of action must be a political set of activities that promise to engage the educator in the activity of liberation, of self and others, if it is to be truly educative. What is presented below is one such agenda, formulated on a class analysis of society which we believe is a potentially productive and progressive movement toward liberation from this viewpoint.

This agenda is predicated on the belief that educators must:

1. Protect their own living standards and their democratic rights, and in order to do this they must distinguish between the struggle based on analysis of class on one hand and liberal reformism on the other. Further, they must unite as broadly as possible with other educators, with students, and with working class and liberation oriented organizations on the *basis* of the principles of class analysis.

2. In order to carry forward their professional work they must raise the demand for:

a. Democracy for students in the schools;

b. A curriculum that is designed to serve the interests of the dominated—the broad working class; and

c. The right to link directly and concretely the education of students with the education and the democratic struggle of the wage-earning and salaried working class.

While the details of action will vary from situation to situation, the following general categories of action are probably appropriate for any "public" school educator:

1. Develop in your school a core of 3 or 4 of the most progressive teachers, initially for the purpose of studying your school from the point of view of whose interests are expressed in the program. For example, begin to examine such data as the relative variance in achievement of lower class and other children. Ask in whose interests the testing program operates. Examine materials, methods, and school policies for differential group bias in relation to the interest structure. Look at educational reform and research projects and reports to reveal the interest base embedded in the implicit assumptions of the proposals and conclusions.

2. Encourage the most progressive students you know to form a group to study and prepare a report upon the presence and/or absence of democracy for students in the school. Involve yourself in the student rights movement, and serve as a resource person for examining the concrete mechanisms in school which abridge student rights. Encourage students to ask and answer "In whose interest?" are these policies or procedures.

3. As the study on dominant class interests progresses, bring your findings to the most progressive parents, and expand your core group to include these parents. Focus discussion both on the school and the broad parallels to these circumstances found in society at large.

4. Bring your work to the attention of educators in other schools through the teachers union and other professional organizations. Encourage the formation of groups like yours in other schools. Plan to meet to compare findings.

5. When investigation at several schools in the area is sufficiently advanced to do so confidently, begin to expose the class content and context of your school program publicly—for example, at PTA and teachers union meetings. Form a group in the union or teacher organization to carry the study forward.

6. Through parents, enlist the help of both community people and members of working class organizations, and establish curriculum committees specifically to develop curriculum based on the interest of the broad community of the working class. This must not be some currently typical "career education" package, but must include as minimal demands:

a. The teaching of modern history focused upon the struggles of Western dominated "third world" countries, the working class, the oppressed national minorities, and women against exploitation

b. Full equality for the language and culture of oppressed national minorities

c. Concrete investigation of the social class relations in the area of the schools' population

d. Instruction in the fundamentals of socioeconomic analysis of social relations

e. Development of cultural activities specifically aimed at the acceptance and validation of traditional working class culture.

7. Establish close links between your developing organization and the developing student organization, including joint meetings and joint presentations at PTA, school board, and other public meetings.

8. Develop close links between your organization and working class and community organizations to which parents in your school area belong. This also should include joint presentations, as well as the planning of ways for students, as part of their regular school work, to participate in community action against attacks on living standards and democratic rights.

9. Establish an area-wide committee of teachers to investigate and report upon the wage structure of teachers and the situation with regard to their democratic rights. Formulate demands on the basis of this report.

10. Establish an area-wide committee, composed of teachers, students, parents, and representatives of progressive community, working class, national minority, and women's organizations to coordinate:

a. Plans for putting forward demands for democracy for staff and students in the schools; for a curriculum based on the interests of the dominated groups in society; for the linking of students' education directly and practically to the struggle for liberation; and for protection of the living standards and democratic rights of teachers.

b. A plan for the broadest possible dissemination, through leaflets, newsletters, and meetings, of information and analysis showing the relations among these demands, the relation of these demands to the demands of various sectors of the community, the relation of all these demands to the basic class structure of society, and the necessity to form a united front among all dominated groups against the increasingly apparent move toward more centralized and rigid control by the power structure.

Addenda

A crisis of major proportions in our society is with us now and before us in the foreseeable future. For the vast majority of people, this could well mean: (a) a loss of political liberties, and (b) an attack on our standard of living. The crisis is symbolized by rampant inflation, currency and gold market manipulation and speculation, dollar devaluation, energy and mineral crisis, world food shortages, and industrially profit-motivated ecological disasters.

The life style characterized by increasing material consumption of nonessential goods, personal striving for more "things," and self-identification with "middle-class" values is in imminent danger of collapsing in the near future, most probably as a result of a catastrophic deflation (or depression) of the material well being of the vast majority of people in our society. The era of unilateral economic policy and measured success in a growing Gross National Product will shortly be a thing of the past.

A Futurists Conference convened by ASCD under Past President Harold G. Shane's leadership in August 1973 resulted in general agreement that this crisis is coming, and that the options or alternatives open to American society (short of nuclear war) are: (a) the development of a "friendly fascist state"; and (b) the development of a society of pluralistic life styles or participatory intentional communities. Essentially the two directions characterize the move toward a more centralized, ordered, and restrictive society focused on control and allocation of diminished affluence; versus a change toward the development of a society which seeks its rewards through human relationships rather than material well being, per se; most probably in the form of pluralistic participation in intentional communities with minitechnology tented under a broadly federated and justly regulated superstructure.

In either eventuality there is a tremendous urgency that members of the profession and society at large be prepared to act and move courageously toward the ends they value. We may well have an opportunity to move and reform schooling (as the material nexus unravels) in ways and to degrees that we have previously not imagined possible. But by all means we must be prepared with firm values, attitudes, and reasonable concepts of strategies and programs in order to move progressively during this coming crisis. We must not fall into the general syndrome of our characteristic response— "too little and too late." Even though, as this volume itself has demonstrated, there is, and will no doubt continue to be, conflict and disagreement among the individuals and groups of people who are struggling to recreate our institutions, one thing should be clear. Each of us must ask "What is to be done?", "In whose interest?"; and then, each one of us must take honestly the question, "What am *I* to do?"

Additional References

Charles Baudelaire. *Paris Spleen*. Louise Varese, translator. New York: New Directions Press, 1947.

Daniel Bell. "Crisis in Education." In: *Confrontation: The Student Rebellion and the Universities*. Daniel Bell and Irving Kristol, editors. New York: Basic Books, Inc., Publishers, 1969.

Richard Bernstein. *Praxis and Action: Contemporary Philosophies of Human Activity*. Philadelphia: University of Pennsylvania Press, 1971.

Arthur Bestor. *Educational Wastelands: The Retreat From Learning in Our Public Schools*. Urbana: University of Illinois Press, 1953.

John Franklin Bobbitt. *The Curriculum*. New York: Arno Press, 1971. (Copyright 1918).

Sarane S. Boocock. *Introduction to the Sociology of Learning*. Boston: Houghton Mifflin Company, 1972.

Jerome S. Bruner. *Process of Education*. Cambridge: Harvard University Press, 1960.

James Samuel Coleman *et al. Equality of Educational Opportunity*. U.S. Department of Health, Education, and Welfare, Office of Education. Washington: United States Government Printing Office, 1966.

Arthur W. Combs, editor. *Perceiving, Behaving, Becoming*. Yearbook. Washington, D.C.: Association for Supervision and Curriculum Development, 1962.

George S. Counts. *Dare the Schools Build A New Social Order*. New York: Arno Press, Inc., 1969. (Reprint of 1932 edition).

Lawrence A. Cremin. *Transformation of the School*. New York: Alfred A. Knopf, Inc., 1961.

Delmo Della-Dora and James E. House, editors. *Education for An Open Society*. Yearbook. Washington, D.C.: Association for Supervision and Curriculum Development, 1974.

Amitai Etzioni. *Studies in Social Change*. New York: Holt, Rinehart and Winston, Inc., 1966.

Shulamith Firestone. *The Dialectic of Sex: The Case For Feminist Revolution.* New York: Bantam Books, Inc., 1971.

John I. Goodlad and M. Frances Klein. *Behind The Classroom Door.* Worthington, Ohio: Charles A. Jones Publishing Co., 1970.

Vernon Haubrich, editor. *Freedom, Bureaucracy, and Schooling.* Yearbook. Washington, D.C.: Association for Supervision and Curriculum Development, 1971.

Max Horkheimer. *Critical Theory: Selected Essays.* Matthew J. O'Connell, translator. New York: Herder & Herder, Inc., 1972.

David Hulbrud. *This Happened in Pasadena.* New York: Macmillan Publishing Co., Inc., 1951.

Christopher Jencks. *Inequality.* New York: Basic Books, Inc., Publishers, 1972.

Albert Lynd. *Quackery in the Public Schools.* New York: Grossett and Dunlap, Inc., 1956.

Frederick Mosteller and Daniel P. Moynihan, editors. *On Equality of Educational Opportunity.* New York: Random House, Inc., 1972.

Friedrich Wilhelm Nietzsche. *Schopenhauer as Educator.* James W. Hillesheim, translator. Chicago: Henry Regnery Company, 1965.

Joseph Mayer Rice. "The Futility of the Spelling Grind." *The Forum,* Vol. 23, 1897.

Zalmen Slesinger. *Education and the Class Struggle: A Critical Examination of the Liberal Educator's Program for Social Reconstruction.* New York: Covici-Friede, 1937.

B. Othanel Smith et al. *Fundamentals of Curriculum Development.* New York: Harcourt Brace Jovanovich, Inc., revised edition 1969.

Mortimer Smith. *And Madly Teach.* Chicago: Henry Regnery Company, 1969.

Mortimer B. Smith. *Diminished Mind: A Study of Planned Mediocrity in Our Public Schools.* Westport, Connecticut: Greenwood Press, Inc., reprint of 1959 edition.

Florence Stratemeyer et al. *Developing A Curriculum for Modern Living.* New York: Teachers College Press, 1947.

Paul Woodring. *Let's Talk Sense About Our Schools.* New York: McGraw-Hill Book Company, 1953.

Readings

Paul Adams *et al. Children's Rights.* New York: Praeger Publishers, 1972.

Saul Alinsky. *Rules for Radicals.* New York: Random House, Inc., 1971.

Philippe Ariés. *Centuries of Childhood.* New York: Random House, Inc., 1962.

Assembly Office of Research. *California Children: Who Cares? A Progress Report on the California Assembly Symposium on Services to Children and Youth.* Sacramento: the Assembly Office, March 1974.

Charles Baudelaire. *Paris Spleen.* Louise Varese, translator. New York: New Directions Press, 1947.

Bay Area Radical Teachers' Organizing Collective. *No More Teachers' Dirty Looks* 3 (1). San Francisco, California: the Collective.

Bay Area Radical Teachers' Organizing Collective. *Education and Corporate Capitalism.* Boston: New England Free Press.

John Beecher. *Collected Poems, 1924-1974.* New York: Macmillan Publishing Co., Inc., 1974.

Stephen Berg and S. J. Marks, editors. *About Women.* Greenwich, Connecticut: Fawcett Publications, Inc., 1973.

Samuel Bowies and Herbert Gintis. "The IQ Ideology." *This Magazine Is All About Schools* 6 (4); Winter 1972.

William G. Buss. *Legal Aspects of Crime Investigation in the Public Schools.* Topeka: National Organization on Legal Problems of Education, 1971.

Henry Butler, Jr., *et al. Legal Aspects of Student Records.* Topeka: National Organization on Legal Problems of Education, 1972.

Melvin A. Butler *et al.* "Students' Rights to Their Own Language." A special issue of *College Composition and Communication* 25; Fall 1974.

John Buttrick. "Who Goes to University in Toronto." *This Magazine Is All About Schools* 6 (2); Summer 1972.

Maren Lockwood Carden. *The New Feminist Movement.* New York: Russell Sage Foundation, 1974.

Martin Carnoy. *Education as Cultural Imperialism.* New York: David McKay Co., Inc., 1974.

Center for Law and Education. *Classification Materials.* Cambridge, Massachusetts: the Center, 1973.

Center for Law and Education. *Inequality in Education.* No. 14. Cambridge, Massachusetts: the Center, July 1973.

Center for Law and Education. *Student Fees.* Cambridge, Massachusetts: the Center, 1972.

Center for Law and Education. *Student Rights Litigation Packet.* Cambridge, Massachusetts: the Center, 1972.

Center for Law and Education. *Title I Litigation Materials.* Cambridge, Massachusetts: the Center, 1972.

Centerpeace. Issue 15. 57 Hayes Street, Cambridge, Massachusetts, January-March 1973.

John Chambers, translator. "Selections from the Quebec Teachers White Paper on Socio-Political Action." *This Magazine Is All About Schools* 6 (1); Spring 1972.

O. M. Collective. *The Organizers Manual.* New York: Bantam Books, Inc., 1971.

Lewis A. Coser. *The Functions of Social Conflict.* New York: The Free Press, 1956.

Barbara M. Cross, editor. *The Educated Woman in America.* New York: Teachers College Press, 1965.

Simone de Beauvoir. *The Second Sex.* H. M. Parshley, translator and editor. New York: Alfred A. Knopf, Inc., 1952.

Regis Debray. *Revolution in the Revolution.* Baltimore: Penguin Books, Inc., 1967.

J. W. B. Douglas. *The Home and the School.* New York: Ballantine Books, Inc., 1972.

Jerome Ellison. *A Serious Call to an American (R)evolution.* Berkeley, California: Berkeley Medallion Books, 1967.

Edcentric. Issue No. 26. Eugene, Oregon: October 1973.

Educational Leadership 31 (2): 97-192; November 1973. Theme issue on "Women and Education."

The Emma Willard Task Force on Education. *Sexism in Education.* Minneapolis: the Task Force, 1971.

Friedrich Engels. Eleanor Burke Leacock, editor. *The Origin of the Family, Private Property and the State.* New York: International Publishers Company, Inc., 1942.

Friedrich Engels. *Socialism, Utopian and Scientific.* New York: International Publishers Company, Inc., 1935.

Shulamith Firestone. *The Dialectic of Sex: The Case for Feminist Revolution.* New York: Bantam Books, Inc., 1971.

Joseph François. "Canarsie: The Great Sellout—A View from

Within." *The People Against Racism in Education Paper.* September-October 1973.

Paulo Freire. "Cultural Action for Freedom." *Harvard Education Review.* Vol. 40: May-August 1970.

Paulo Freire. *Pedagogy of the Oppressed.* New York: Herder & Herder, Inc., 1970.

Edgar Z. Friedenberg. *The Dignity of Youth and Other Atavisms.* Boston: Beacon Press, 1966.

Erich Fromm. *The Revolution of Hope.* New York: Bantam Books, Inc., 1968.

Dale Gaddy. *Rights and Freedoms of Public School Students.* Topeka: National Organization on Legal Problems of Education, 1971.

Alan Gartner, Colin Greer, and Frank Reismann. *The New Assault on Equality: IQ and Social Stratification.* New York: Harper & Row, Publishers, Perennial Library, 1974.

Paul Goodman. *Compulsory Mis-education.* New York: Vintage Books, 1962.

Vivian Gornick and Barbara K. Moran, editors. *Woman in Sexist Society, Studies in Power and Powerlessness.* New York: Basic Books, Inc., Publishers, 1971.

Allen Graubard. *Free The Children.* New York: Vintage Books, 1972.

Germaine Greer. *The Female Eunuch.* New York: McGraw-Hill Book Company, 1971.

Ronald and Beatrice Gross, editors. *Radical School Reform.* New York: Simon & Schuster, Inc., 1969.

Guidelines for the Collection, Maintenance, and Dissemination of Pupil Records. New York: Russell Sage Foundation, n.d.

Jürgen Habermas. *Toward a Rational Society.* Boston: Beacon Press, 1970.

Barbara Grizzuti Harrison. *Unlearning the Lie, Sexism in School.* New York: William Morrow and Company, Inc., 1974.

The Rights of Children, Parts I and II. Cambridge, Massachusetts: Harvard Education Review, Reprint No. 9, 1974.

Max Horkheimer. *Critical Theory: Selected Essays.* Matthew J. O'Connell, translator. New York: Herder & Herder, Inc., 1972.

Karen Horney. *Feminine Psychology.* New York: W. W. Norton & Co., Inc., 1967.

Joan Huber, editor. *Changing Women in a Changing Society.* Chicago: The University of Chicago Press, 1973.

Ivan Illich *et al. After Deschooling, What?* Alan Gartner, Colin Greer, and Frank Reissman, editors. New York: Harper & Row, Publishers, Perennial Library, 1971.

Ivan Illich. *Deschooling Society.* New York: Harrow Books, Harper & Row, Publishers, 1972.

S. Kahn. *How People Get Power.* New York: McGraw-Hill Book Company, 1970.

Clarence Karier, Paul Violas, and Joel Spring. *Roots of Crisis.* Chicago: Rand McNally & Company, 1973.

Nell Keddie. *The Myth of Cultural Deprivation.* Baltimore: Penguin Books, Inc., 1973.

Robert F. Kennedy Memorial. *Captive Voices.* New York: Schocken Books, Inc., 1973.

Herbert Kohl. "The Politics of Jargon." *The Teacher Paper* 4 (3): 9-16; February 1972.

Elizabeth Koontz. *The Best Kept Secret of the Past 5,000 Years: Women Are Ready for Leadership in Education.* Bloomington, Indiana: The Phi Delta Kappa Educational Foundation, 1972.

Jonathan Kozol. "Look What They've Done to Helen Keller." *The Teacher Paper* 6 (2): 19-25; December 1973.

Jonathan Kozol. "Schools for Survival." *This Magazine Is All About Schools* 5 (4); Fall/Winter 1971.

V. I. Lenin. *Imperialism, The Highest Stage of Capitalism.* Peking: Foreign Languages Press, 1973.*

V. I. Lenin. *Karl Marx.* Peking: Foreign Languages Press, 1970.*

V. I. Lenin. *On the National and Colonial Questions.* Peking: Foreign Languages Press, 1970.*

V. I. Lenin. *The State and Revolution.* Peking: Foreign Languages Press, 1973.*

The Emancipation of Women. From the writings of V. I. Lenin. Preface by Nadezhda K. Krupskaya. New York: International Publishers Company, Inc., 1972.

Alan Levine et al. *The Rights of Students.* New York: Avon Books, 1973.

Loren Lind and John Buttrick. "Class Bias and Bureaucracy in Ontario." *This Magazine Is All About Schools* 5 (4); Fall/Winter 1971.

Loren Lind. "The Rise of Bureaucracy in Ontario Schools." *This Magazine Is All About Schools* 6 (2): 104-119; Summer 1972.

James Lorimer. "Canadian Textbooks and the American Knowledge Industry." *This Magazine Is All About Schools* 5 (3); Summer 1971.

Ellen Lurie. *How To Change the Schools.* New York: Vintage Books, 1970.

Staughton Lynd. *Intellectual Origins of American Radicalism.* New York: Vintage Books, 1969.

Mao Tse-tung. "Analysis of Classes in Chinese Society." *Selected Works of Mao Tse-tung.* Peking: Foreign Languages Press, 1970.*

Mao Tse-tung. "On Contradiction." *Selected Works of Mao Tse-tung.* Peking: Foreign Languages Press, 1970.*

Karl Marx. *Manifesto of the Communist Party.* Peking: Foreign Languages Press, 1972.*

* Available through China Books & Periodicals, 125 Fifth Avenue, New York, N.Y. 10003.

Karl Marx and V. I. Lenin. *The Civil War in France.* New York: International Publishers Company, Inc., 1968.

Selections from the writing of Karl Marx, Friedrich Engels, V. I. Lenin, Joseph Stalin. *The Woman Question.* New York: International Publishers Company, Inc., 1951.

Edwin Mason. *Collaborative Learning.* New York: Agathon Press, Inc., 1972.

Patricia Michaels. "Parents in the School: Community Control in Harlem." *This Magazine Is All About Schools* 4 (4); Fall 1970.

Patricia Michaels. "Teaching Rebellion at Union Springs." *This Magazine Is All About Schools* 4 (4); Fall 1970.

Kate Millett. *Sexual Politics.* Garden City: Doubleday & Company, Inc., 1970.

A. Morrison and D. McIntyre. *Schools and Socialization.* Baltimore: Penguin Books, Inc., 1971.

Friedrich Wilhelm Nietzsche. *Schopenhauer as Educator.* James W. Hillesheim, translator. Chicago: Henry Regnery Company, 1965.

Michael Nussbaum. *Student Legal Rights.* New York: Harper & Row, Publishers, 1970.

The Park School Community Council Brief. "Class Bias in Toronto Schools." *This Magazine Is All About Schools* 5 (4); Fall/Winter 1971.

Robert E. Phay. *Suspension and Expulsion of Public School Students.* Topeka: National Organization on Legal Problems of Education, 1971.

Wilhelm Reich. *Character Analysis.* New York: Noonday Press, 1945.

Wilhelm Reich. *The Invasion of Compulsory Sex-Morality.* New York: Noonday Press, 1970.

Wilhelm Reich. *The Mass Psychology of Fascism.* New York: Noonday Press, 1970.

Wilhelm Reich. *The Sexual Revolution.* New York: Noonday Press, 1969.

John Reid. *The Best Little Boy in the World.* New York: G. P. Putnam's Sons, 1973.

Everett Reimer. *School Is Dead.* New York: Doubleday & Company, Inc., 1973.

Alan Reitman *et al. Corporal Punishment in Public Schools.* New York: ACLU Reports, 1972.

Saru Repo, editor. *This Book Is About Schools.* New York: Vintage Books, 1970.

Edmund Reutter. *Legal Aspects of Control of Student Activities by School Authorities.* Topeka: National Organization on Legal Problems of Education, 1970.

Len Richmond and Gary Noguera, editors. *The Gay Liberation Book.* San Francisco: Ramparts Press, Inc., 1973.

Arthur Rimbaud. *A Season in Hell.* Louise Varese, translator. New York: New Directions Press, 1945.

Arthur Rimbaud. *Illuminations.* Louise Varese, translator. New York: New Directions Press, 1946.

Don Robertson and Marion Steele. *The Halls of Yearning.* San Francisco: Harper & Row, Publishers, Canfield Press, 1971.

Michelle Zimbalist Rosaldo and Louise Lamphere, editors. *Woman, Culture, and Society.* Stanford, California: Stanford University Press, 1974.

Susan C. Ross. *The Rights of Women.* New York: Avon Books, 1973.

Betty Roszak and Theodore Roszak, editors. *Masculine/Feminine: Readings in Sexual Mythology and the Liberation of Women.* New York: Harper & Row, Publishers, 1969.

Sheila Rowbotham. *Women, Resistance and Revolution.* New York: Vintage Books, 1974.

School Review. Special issue: "Women and Education." 80 (2); February 1972.

Ruth Sidel. *Women and Child Care in China.* New York: Hill and Wang (Division of Farrar, Straus & Giroux, Inc.), 1972.

C. H. Sisson, translator. *The Poetry of Catullus.* New York: The Viking Press, Inc., 1966.

Nobuo Shimahara and Adam Scrupski, editors. *Social Forces and Schooling.* New York: David McKay Company, Inc., 1975.

Eleanor Smollett. "The Middle Class and the Open Classroom." *This Magazine Is All About Schools* 7 (4); January 1974.

Joseph Stalin. *Dialectical and Historical Materialism.* New York: International Publishers Company, Inc., 1940.

Joseph Stalin. *Foundations of Leninism.* Peking: Foreign Languages Press, 1970.*

Annie Stein. "A Hard Look at the Board's Accountability Plan." *The P.A.R.E. Paper.* September-October 1973.

David Tabakow. "How Do You Really Grade?" *This Magazine Is All About Schools* 6 (2); Summer 1972.

Training Manual on Public School Life. New York: School Defense Network, 1969.

Charles A. Valentine. *Culture and Poverty.* Chicago: University of Chicago Press, 1968.

Miriam Wasserman, editor. *Demystifying School.* New York: Praeger Publishers, 1974.

Miriam Wasserman. "Respectable Revolutions." *The Teacher Paper* 4 (3): 25-29; February 1972.

Miriam Wasserman. "School Mythology and the Education of Oppression." *This Magazine Is All About Schools* 5 (3); Summer 1971.

Mel Watkins. "Learning to Move Left." *This Magazine Is All About Schools* 6 (1); Spring 1972.

* Available through China Books & Periodicals, 125 Fifth Avenue, New York, N.Y. 10003.

Bruce Wasserstein and Mark J. Green, editors. *With Justice for Some.* Boston: Beacon Press, 1970.

Grant Wetzel and Robert Yourasbita. "School Building and the Politics of Technology." *This Magazine Is All About Schools* 5 (4); Fall/Winter 1971.

Albert E. Wilkerson, editor. *The Rights of Children.* Philadelphia: Temple University Press, 1973.

"Women's Higher Education: Some Unanswered Questions." Prepared by Esther M. Westervelt. Report of a Wingspread Conference. Racine, Wisconsin: The Johnson Foundation, March 1972.

"Student and Youth Organizing." *Youth Liberation Pamphlet.* Ann Arbor, Michigan, 1973.

Notes About the Authors

Michael W. Apple is an Associate Professor in the Department of Curriculum and Instruction at the University of Wisconsin, Madison. He is active in the student rights movement and has served as a consultant in court cases involving politically active teachers. Professor Apple is the author of articles and monographs in curriculum theory and development on such topics as ideology and curriculum thought, the hidden curriculum, and student rights. His most recent publications include *Educational Evaluation: Analysis and Responsibility* and *Schooling and the Rights of Children.*

William Burton is Secretary to the Board of the North Carolina Center for Student Rights, and is also a full-time consultant for the School Desegregation Project of the Southern Regional Council. His area of particular interest is the politics of curriculum and schooling.

Dwayne Huebner, after beginning his academic career in the physical sciences, became an elementary school teacher. In his attempt to better understand elementary education, he did advanced study at the University of Wisconsin in the behavioral sciences and education. Since then his own study has led him into philosophy, theology, and recently critical theory. His college and university career has included teaching in a preservice education program at Northern Illinois University and teaching and advising in graduate programs in curriculum and teaching at Teachers College, Columbia University. At Teachers College, he was also Principal of the Agnes Russell Elementary School.

James B. Macdonald, Co-Chairperson of the 1975 Yearbook Committee, is Distinguished Professor of Education at the University of North Carolina, Greensboro. He is former Chairman of the Department of Curriculum, University of Wisconsin at Madison. He has also taught at the University of London, the University of Texas, and New York University. He has served as Chairman of the ASCD Research Commission and of the Publications Committee, and is a member of the ASCD Executive Council.

John S. Mann is Associate Professor of Elementary Education, University of New Mexico, Albuquerque. He taught at Johns Hopkins University before moving to the University of New Mexico. He has been an active member of ASCD for seven years.

Esther Zaret, Co-Chairperson of the 1975 Yearbook Committee, has been an educator with varying functions over the past twenty-five years: mother; elementary school teacher; researcher; university professor; and, most recently (1973-74), Associate Dean for Graduate Programs at Bank Street College of Education. During 1974-75 she is treating herself to a "sabbatical" for reflection and action toward integrating her previously fragmented roles as woman/educator/social change agent.

ASCD 1975 Yearbook Committee Members

James B. Macdonald, *Co-Chairperson and Co-Editor*
Distinguished Professor of Education
University of North Carolina, Greensboro

Esther Zaret, *Co-Chairperson and Co-Editor*
Milwaukee, Wisconsin

Michael Apple
Associate Professor, Department of Curriculum and Instruction
University of Wisconsin, Madison

Dwayne Huebner
Professor of Education
Teachers College, Columbia University, New York

John S. Mann
Associate Professor, Elementary Education
University of New Mexico, Albuquerque

William Burton
Education Consultant
Southern Regional Council
Atlanta, Georgia

ASCD Board of Directors

as of November 15, 1974

Executive Council, 1974-75

President: Glenys G. Unruh, Assistant Superintendent for Curriculum and Instruction, School District of University City, Missouri

President-Elect: Delmo Della-Dora, Professor and Chairperson, Department of Teacher Education, California State University, Hayward

Immediate Past President: Harold G. Shane, University Professor of Education, School of Education, Indiana University, Bloomington

Mitsuo Adachi, Director, Foreign Contracts Office, College of Education, University of Hawaii, Honolulu

Barbara Day, Coordinator of Early Childhood Education, University of North Carolina, Chapel Hill

Sara M. Davis, Professor, Elementary Education, University of Alabama, University

Gerald Firth, Professor and Chairperson, Curriculum and Supervision Department, University of Georgia, Athens

Richard L. Foster, Director, Berkeley Health Project, Berkeley, California

James E. House, Jr., Consultant, Secondary Education, Wayne County Intermediate School District, Detroit, Michigan

Charles G. Kingston, Jr., Principal, Thomas Fowler Junior High School, Tigard, Oregon

James B. Macdonald, Distinguished Professor of Education, University of North Carolina, Greensboro

Elizabeth S. Randolph, Administrative Assistant for School Operations, Charlotte–Mecklenburg Schools, Charlotte, North Carolina

Bette W. Treadwell, Rockefeller Foundation Fellow, Washington, D.C.

Board Members Elected at Large

Leslee J. Bishop, University of Georgia, Athens (1976)

Julianna Boudreaux, New Orleans Public Schools, Louisiana (1977)

John E. Codwell, Houston Independent School District, Texas (1975)

Joseph W. Crenshaw, State Department of Education, Tallahassee, Florida (1977)

Grace S. Epps, Robeson County Schools, Lumberton, North Carolina, (1975)

C. Glen Hass, University of Florida, Gainesville (1976)

Lucille G. Jordan, Atlanta Public Schools, Georgia (1978)

Edward A. Karns, Parma Public Schools, Ohio (1977)

Milton Kimpson, Community Relations Council, Greater Columbia Chamber of Commerce, Columbia, South Carolina (1977)

Chon LaBrier, Dulce Independent School, Dulce, New Mexico (1978)

Wilma S. Longstreet, University of Michigan, Flint (1975)

Barbara T. Mason, Queens College, City University of New York, Flushing (1976)

John E. McGill, University of Illinois, Urbana (1975)

Norman V. Overly, Indiana University, Bloomington (1978)

James A. Phillips, Jr., Kent State University, Kent, Ohio (1977)

James Raths, University of Illinois, Urbana (1978)

Vincent R. Rogers, University of Connecticut, Storrs (1976)

Dolores Silva, Temple University, Philadelphia, Pennsylvania (1978)

Bette W. Treadwell, Rockefeller Foundation Fellow, Washington, D.C. (1976)

Unit Representatives to the Board of Directors
(Each Unit's President is listed first; others follow in alphabetical order.)

Alabama: Alvis T. Harthern, University of Montevallo, Montevallo; Mildred Ellisor, Auburn University, Auburn; Dorthea Grace Rockarts, University of Alabama, University.

Arizona: Jayne Miller, Public Schools, Phoenix; James J. Jelinek, Arizona State University, Tempe; Herbert B. Wilson, University of Arizona, Tucson.

Arkansas: Jimmie B. Dyer, Public Schools, North Little Rock; Calvin G. Patterson, Public Schools, Fort Smith.

California (liaison): Arthur L. Costa, Sacramento State University, Sacramento; Lewie Burnett, California State University, Hayward; Jon Slezak, Public Schools, Pleasanton; A. Renee L. Rasmussen, San Diego.

Colorado: Alice DeBoer, Public Schools, Aurora; Robert C. McKean, University of Colorado, Boulder; P. L. Schmelzer, Public Schools, Ft. Collins.

Delaware: William J. Bailey, University of Delaware, Newark; Catherine Y. Bonney, Public Schools, Newark.

District of Columbia: Inez Wood, E. A. Clark School; Bessie D. Etheridge, Spingarn Instructional Unit; Lorraine H. Whitlock, Woodson Senior High School.

Florida: James L. Gant, Florida State University, Tallahassee; Aquilina C. Howell, Leon County Public Schools, Tallahassee; Harry F. McComb, Broward County Public Schools, Ft. Lauderdale; Patrick F. Mooney, Dade County Public Schools, Miami; Evelyn W. Sharp, Bethune-Cookman College, Daytona Beach.

Georgia: Edith E. Grimsley, University of Georgia, Athens; Harold T. Johnson, Georgia Southwestern College, Americus; John H. Lounsbury, Georgia State College for Women, Milledgeville.

Hawaii: Sigfried Ramler, Punahou School, Honolulu; Virgie Chattergy, University of Hawaii, Honolulu.

Idaho: Norma J. Sadler, Boise State University, Boise; David A. Carroll, Public Schools, Boise.

Illinois: Louise E. Dieterle, Illinois State University, Bloomington; Marlin Baxter, Public Schools, Moline; Leone Bergfield, Litchfield School District #12, Litchfield; Margaret Carroll, Northern Illinois University, DeKalb; Donald R. Frost, Leyden High School, Northlake; Blanche Martin, Public Schools, Rockford; Donald W. Nylin, Public Schools, Aurora; Mildred Hindman Phegley, Public Schools, Collinsville.

Indiana: Sister Elaine Kohn, Central Catholic Education Complex, Indianapolis; Donna Delph, Purdue University, Calumet Campus, Hammond; Charles E. Kline, Purdue University, South Campus Courts, West Lafayette; James H. McElhinney, Ball State University, Muncie.

Iowa: Robert G. Wrider, Public Schools, Waterloo; Horace S. Hoover, Community School District, Dubuque; Frank Nugent, Johnston Community School, Johnston.

Kansas: Paul H. Koehn, Unified School District #333, Concordia; Walter L. Davies, Public Schools, Kansas City; Harlan J. Trennepohl, Kansas State University, Manhattan.

Kentucky: Billie Jean Cawood, Harlan County Public Schools, Harlan; William Bolton, Clark County Public Schools, Winchester; J. R. Ogletree, University of Kentucky, Lexington.

Louisiana: Edwin H. Friedrich, Public Schools, New Orleans; Katye Lee Posey, Caddo Parish Schools, Shreveport; Emelie M. Willkomm, Public Schools, New Orleans.

Maryland: Raymond E. Clarke, Public Schools, Chestertown; Benjamin P. Ebersole, Baltimore County Public Schools, Towson; Robert E. Hess, Public Schools, Frederick; L. Morris McClure, University of Maryland, College Park.

Massachusetts: Arthur F. Baker, Bridgewater State College, Bridgewater; Gilbert W. Berry, Maria Hastings School, Lexington; C. Louis Cedrone, Public Schools, Westwood; Paul V. Congdon, Springfield College, Springfield.

Michigan: LaBarbara A. Gragg, Wayne County Intermediate School District, Detroit; William Cansfield, Public Schools, Mt. Clemens; Morrel J. Clute, Wayne State University, Detroit; Stuart C. Rankin, Public Schools, Detroit; Virginia Sorenson, Western Michigan University, Grand Rapids; Jack Wickert, Public Schools, Kalamazoo.

Minnesota: Donald J. Christensen, Independent School District #196, Rosemount; Stan Gilbertson, Independent School District #271, Bloomington; Floyd E. Keller, State Department of Education, St. Paul.

Mississippi: James V. McCullouch, Public Schools, Meridian; Norvel Burkett, Mississippi State University, State College.

Missouri: Max Wolfrum, Public Schools, Webster Groves; Richard King, State Department of Education, Jefferson City; Patricia Rocklage, Public Schools, St. Louis; Howard Lowe, Public Schools, Springfield.

Montana: Warren L. Morehouse, Public Schools, Helena; Lloyd B. Ellingsen, Public Schools, Billings.

Nebraska: Niels C. Wodder, Westside Community Schools, Omaha; Gerald Bryant, Public Schools, Grand Island; J. Jay Planteen, Public Schools, Omaha.

Nevada: Mel Kirchner, Washoe County School District, Reno; William K. Moore, Clark County School District, Las Vegas.

New England: Lyman C. Hunt, Jr., The University of Vermont, Burlington; Ashley Gray, University of Maine, Orono; Edward G. Hunt, Rhode Island Health Science Education Council, Cranston; Joan D. Kerelejza, Public Schools, West Hartford.

New Jersey: Arnold D. Tversky, Public Schools, Dover; Kathryn M. Cooper, Public Schools, Ridgewood; Mary Jane Diehl, Monmouth College, Witong Branch; Alma Flagg, Public Schools, Newark; Donald J. Gudaitis, Public Schools, Ringwood; Nicholas Sferrazza, Gloucester Township Public Schools, Blackwood.

New Mexico: Joan M. Craig, Public Schools, Los Alamos; Patricia Christman, Public Schools, Albuquerque; Zella M. Hunter, Public Schools, Roswell.

New York: Peter Incalcaterra, Public Schools, Kingston; Paul Anderson, Public Schools, Baldwinsville; Dianne Gess, Public Schools, Suffern; Helen F. Rice, New York ASCD, Rochester; Thomas A. Schottman, Public Schools, Scotia; Walter R. Suess, Public Schools, Wantagh; Conrad Toepfer, Jr., State University of New York, Buffalo; Gordon E. VanHooft, State Education Department, Albany.

North Carolina: Lucille Bazemore, Bertie County Public Schools; Windsor and Josephine Spaulding, Public Schools, Whiteville; Robert C. Hanes, Chapel Hill–Carrboro City Schools, Chapel Hill; Marcus C. Smith, Public Schools, Salisbury.

Ohio: Thelma D. Schraer, Public Schools, West Chester; Robert J. Alfonso, Kent State University, Kent; Gary H. Deutschlander, Public Schools, Berea; Charles A. Loparo, Public Schools, Brecksville; James K. Uphoff, Wright State University, Celina; Maxwell Werner, Public Schools, Lockland.

Oklahoma: Gene D. Shepherd, University of Oklahoma, Norman; Russell B. Dobson, Oklahoma State University, Stillwater.

Oregon: Max L. Brunton, Public Schools, Portland; Harry Boyd, Public Schools, Ontario; William B. Brewster, Public Schools, Central Point; Charles R. Gengler, Oregon College of Education, Monmouth.

Pennsylvania: Robert V. Flynn, Baldwin-Whitehall School District, Pittsburgh; Kenneth R. Chuska, Peters Township School District, McMurray; Gladys E. Creagmile, Public Schools, Philadelphia; Margaret McFeaters, Slippery Rock State College, Slippery Rock; Henry W. Ray, Bucks County Public Schools, Warminster; Claude P. Swartzbaugh, Jr., Derry Township School District, Hershey.

Puerto Rico: Gladys Davila de Fuente, University of Puerto Rico, Rio Piedras; Ilia Del Toro, University of Puerto Rico, Rio Piedras.

South Carolina: Charles S. Marshall, Public Schools, Lancaster; Ben Carson, Greenville County Public Schools, Greenville; Fred Splittgerber, Wardlaw College, University of South Carolina, Columbia.

South Dakota: Lincoln Henry, Black Hills State College, Spearfish; Signie A. Johnson, Public Schools, Sioux Falls.

Tennessee: Jerry C. McGee, Middle Tennessee State University, Murfreesboro; Mattie R. Crossley, Public Schools, Memphis; Ken Thornton, Lakeview Educational Cooperative, Jefferson City.

Texas: Mary Wakefield, Sam Houston State University, Huntsville; R. C. Bradley, North Texas State University, Denton; Dorothy Davidson, Texas Education Agency, Austin; Dwane Russell, Stephen F. Austin State University, Nacogdoches; James L. Williamson, Pan American University, Edinburg.

Utah: Carma M. Hales, U-Sail Project, Salt Lake City; Nellie T. Higbee, Public Schools, Murray.

Virginia: Hilda P. Pendergrass, Public Schools, Goochland; William J. Hopkins, Sussex County Public Schools, Sussex; Margaret B. Moss, State Department of Education, Richmond; Gennette Nygard, Public Schools, Arlington.

Washington: Richard L. Stimpson, Eastmont School District #206, East Wenatchee; Donald Hair, State Office of Public Instruction, Olympia.

West Virginia: Wilhelmina Ashworth, Fayette County Schools, Fayetteville; Lucille Heflebower, Jefferson County Schools, Charles Town; Betty Livengood, Mineral County Schools, Keyser.

Wisconsin: Jim E. Claude, Public Schools, Black River Falls; Myron Anderson, Public Schools, Whitefish Bay; William Ernst, Department of Public Instruction, Madison; Robert Krey, University of Wisconsin–Superior, Superior.

Wyoming: Edward E. Paradis, University of Wyoming, Laramie; Laurence A. Walker, University of Wyoming, Laramie.

ASCD Review Council, 1974-75

Alvin D. Loving, Sr., House Office Building, Washington, D.C.

M. Karl Openshaw, *Chairman,* Dean, School of Education, University of Colorado, Boulder

Chandos Reid Rice, Boulder, Colorado

William Van Til, Coffman Distinguished Professor in Education, Indiana State University, Terre Haute

Deborah Partridge Wolfe, Professor of Education, Queens College of The City University of New York, Flushing

ASCD Headquarters Staff

Executive Secretary: Gordon Cawelti

Associate Secretary; Editor, ASCD Publications: Robert R. Leeper

Associate Secretary: Geneva Gay

Associate Secretary: Charles A. Speiker

Business Manager: John H. Bralove

Administrative Assistant: Virginia O. Berthy

Staff Assistants:

Elsa Angell

Sarah Arlington

Elizabeth A. Brooks

Cecelia Clayton

Barbara Collins

Caroline Grills

Teola T. Jones

Carvangeline B. Miller

Frances Mindel

Maureen Montgomery

Iris L. Morton

Nancy Olson

Alice H. Powell

Carolyn M. Shell

Barbara J. Sims

Myra K. Taub

ASCD Publications, Spring 1975

Yearbooks

Balance in the Curriculum (610-17274)	$5.00
Education for an Open Society (610-74012)	$8.00
Education for Peace: Focus on Mankind (610-17946)	$7.50
Evaluation as Feedback and Guide (610-17700)	$6.50
Freedom, Bureaucracy, & Schooling (610-17508)	$6.50
Individualizing Instruction (610-17264)	$4.00
Leadership for Improving Instruction (610-17454)	$4.00
Learning and Mental Health in the School (610-17674)	$5.00
Life Skills in School and Society (610-17786)	$5.50
New Insights and the Curriculum (610-17548)	$6.00
A New Look at Progressive Education (610-17812)	$8.00
Schools in Search of Meaning (610-75044)	$8.50
Perceiving, Behaving, Becoming: A New Focus for Education (610-17278)	$5.00
To Nurture Humaneness: Commitment for the '70's (610-17810)	$6.00

Books and Booklets

Action Learning: Student Community Service Projects (611-74018)	$2.50
Bases for World Understanding and Cooperation: Suggestions for Teaching the Young Child (611-17834)	$1.00
Better Than Rating (611-17298)	$2.00
Beyond Jencks: The Myth of Equal Schooling (611-17928)	$2.00
The Changing Curriculum: Mathematics (611-17724)	$2.00
Criteria for Theories of Instruction (611-17756)	$2.00
Curricular Concerns in a Revolutionary Era (611-17852)	$6.00
Curriculum Change: Direction and Process (611-17698)	$2.00
A Curriculum for Children (611-17790)	$3.00
Curriculum Materials 1974 (611-74014)	$2.00
Dare To Care / Dare To Act: Racism and Education (611-17850)	$2.00
Differentiated Staffing (611-17924)	$3.50
Discipline for Today's Children and Youth (611-17314)	$1.50
Early Childhood Education Today (611-17766)	$2.00
Educational Accountability: Beyond Behavioral Objectives (611-17856)	$2.50
Elementary School Mathematics: A Guide to Current Research (611-17752)	$2.75
Elementary School Science: A Guide to Current Research (611-17726)	$2.25
Elementary School Social Studies: A Guide to Current Research (611-17384)	$2.75
Eliminating Ethnic Bias in Instructional Materials: Comment and Bibliography (611-74020)	$3.25
Ethnic Modification of Curriculum (611-17832)	$1.00
Freeing Capacity To Learn (611-17322)	$2.00

Guidelines for Elementary Social Studies (611-17738)	$1.50
Human Variability and Learning (611-17332)	$2.00
The Humanities and the Curriculum (611-17708)	$2.00
Humanizing the Secondary School (611-17780)	$2.75
Improving Educational Assessment & An Inventory of Measures of Affective Behavior (611-17804)	$4.50
Intellectual Development: Another Look (611-17618)	$1.75
International Dimension of Education (611-17816)	$2.25
Interpreting Language Arts Research for the Teacher (611-17846)	$4.00
Language and Meaning (611-17696)	$2.75
Learning More About Learning (611-17310)	$2.00
Linguistics and the Classroom Teacher (611-17720)	$2.75
A Man for Tomorrow's World (611-17838)	$2.25
Middle School in the Making (611-74024)	$5.00
New Dimensions in Learning (611-17336)	$2.00
Nurturing Individual Potential (611-17606)	$2.00
Observational Methods in the Classroom (611-17948)	$3.50
On Early Learning: The Modifiability of Human Potential (611-17842)	$2.00
Open Schools for Children (611-17916)	$3.75
Personalized Supervision (611-17680)	$1.75
Removing Barriers to Humaneness in the High School (611-17848)	$2.50
Reschooling Society: A Conceptual Model (611-17950)	$2.00
The School of the Future—NOW (611-17920)	$3.75
Schools Become Accountable: A PACT Approach (611-74016)	$3.50
Social Studies Education Projects: An ASCD Index (611-17844)	$2.00
Social Studies for the Evolving Individual (611-17952)	$3.00
Strategy for Curriculum Change (611-17666)	$2.00
Student Unrest: Threat or Promise? (611-17818)	$2.75
Supervision: Emerging Profession (611-17796)	$5.00
Supervision in a New Key (611-17926)	$2.50
Supervision: Perspectives and Propositions (611-17732)	$2.00
The Supervisor: Agent for Change in Teaching (611-17702)	$3.25
The Supervisor's Role in Negotiation (611-17798)	$1.00
The Unstudied Curriculum: Its Impact on Children (611-17820)	$2.75
What Are the Sources of the Curriculum? (611-17522)	$1.50
Vitalizing the High School (611-74026)	$3.50
Child Growth Chart (611-17442) min. order 10 for	$2.00

Discounts on quantity orders of same title to single address: 10-49 copies, 10%; 50 or more copies, 15%. Make checks or money orders payable to ASCD. All orders must be prepaid except those on official purchase order forms. Shipping and handling charges will be added to billed purchase orders. **Please be sure to list the stock number of each publication, shown above in parentheses.**

Subscription to **Educational Leadership**—$8.00 a year. ASCD Membership dues: Regular (subscription and yearbook)—$20.00 a year; Comprehensive (includes subscription and yearbook plus other books and booklets distributed during period of the membership)—$30.00 a year.

Order from: **Association for Supervision and Curriculum Development**
Suite 1100, 1701 K Street, N.W., Washington, D.C. 20006

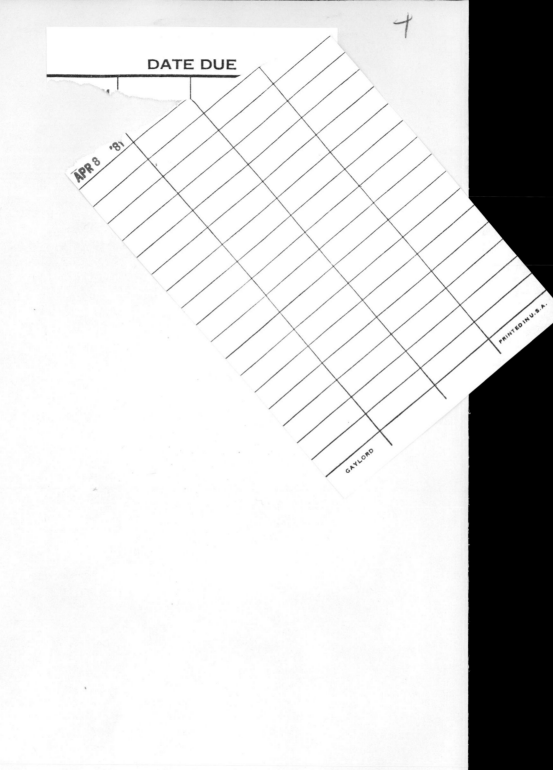

DATE DUE

APR 8 '81

GAYLORD

PRINTED IN U.S.A.